Testimonials

"Reading JoAnn's words are like having a kind and wise companion to guide us through life's joys and struggles. Written with clarity, wisdom, and kindness, this book will be an indispensable support for anyone wishing to live with more awareness, kindness, and presence."

—Mark Coleman, meditation teacher and author of *Awake in the Wild: Mindfulness in Nature as a Path of Self-Discovery* and *Make Peace with Your Mind: How Mindfulness and Compassion Can Free You from Your Inner Critic*

"*Mindful and Intentional Living* is a lovely book filled with gentle wisdom and guidance. Ranging from ancient Buddhist meditations to modern scientific research, the book provides powerful reasons to adopt a compassionate mindfulness practice. With her welcoming voice and stories of struggle and redemption, JoAnn Saccato is a trustworthy guide on the journey of awakening."

—Kevin Griffin, author of *One Breath at a Time: Buddhism and the Twelve Steps* and *Living Kindness: Buddhist Teachings for a Troubled World*

"She is wonderful! During the course of this past year working with JoAnn I faced serious health challenges and at times had lost complete focus of where I was going and what I still wanted to do in this lifetime.

Her coaching and teaching taught me to "pay kind attention to my life," and in the process I learned how to grow into and accept the practice of being in my life while attempting, to the best of my ability, to live my life in the present. I am still a work in progress, but some miracles I now believe just take a little more time than others. Fortunately, I have JoAnn to gently encourage me down the path toward wholeness."

—Anita Swanson-Speake, author of
Slow Hope: The Long Journey Home

"Through JoAnn's teachings I've learned to build a healthy relationship with myself by setting positive intentions and practicing mindfulness. Her book is full of practical suggestions and insights. Hearing JoAnn's personal experiences helped me overcome many obstacles and I'm now able to enrich my spiritual growth where I was once stuck. I use the tools I learned and refer back to the chapters often. Her course was so life changing for me."

—Jennifer Freitas, LMFT (ret.)

"Simple, clear, and compassionate steps are JoAnn's signature in bringing mindful awareness into her reader's lives with this book. With her gentle approach to teaching she brings us to an awareness of how we may be feeding our own stress without realizing it, then smoothly guides us to learn simple tools that help keep us grounded and in a stable and peaceful mind set, even in the face of today's unique stresses. Her personal stories reveal her sincerity in wanting to help those who suffer from mild daily stress to those living with PTSD and uncover a vulnerable history of her own past struggles with finding peaceful stability. Her journey of awakening is an example to her readers that happiness and spiritual awakening are within each of us, lying in wait to be uncovered and released."

—Joanie Lane, Meditation Teacher and Director of
A Positive Light Meditation Center

"JoAnn's wonderful insights, guidance, and inspiration are valuable, regardless of the path one is taking. Her book and courses are a wealth of ideas and practices to make one's life richer and more balanced."

—Kathy Windrem

"There was a time when I thought my solution for discomfort and dysthymia came from outside myself. JoAnn's wonderful book reminds me this is not so. Using simple tools, such as mindfulness and setting intentions, along with a dash of self-discipline, she so gracefully leads me to my loving, open, spacious, and authentic self. I've known JoAnn for nearly twenty years and see her practice what she teaches. Evidence-based mindfulness, along with her other suggested practices, is taking me from unconsciousness to a conscious-filled, mindful and intentionally lived life. If you want to change your life and your perspective for the good—to remember to embrace and revel in each moment mindfully—do read this book!"

—Nancy Perrin, Pulmonary Rehabilitation Coordinator (ret.) and smoking cessation facilitator

"When I first heard of mindfulness, I had no idea what it really was, except that it was probably something like meditation. Seeking relief from anxiety, I decided to take JoAnn's class, of which this book was used as curriculum. The results of undertaking the exercises outlined in the book have been truly astounding! Goodbye anxiety medication and hello mindfulness!

—Steven MacDonald, journalist/graphic artist (ret.)

Mindful and Intentional Living

Mindful and Intentional Living

A Path to Peace, Clarity, and Freedom

JoAnn Saccato

Cover Design by Kathy Wolden

Print information available on the last page.

Rev. date: 07/21/2018

To order additional copies of this book, contact:
Xlibris
1-888-795-4274
www.Xlibris.com
Orders@Xlibris.com
779445

Contents

Including Compassion and Kindness

Clarifying Our Path to Happiness

Deepening Compassion and Kindness

Companioning Us Onward

Acknowledgments and Dedication

To the great winds of creation that bring loving people and circumstances to my life: my lover and best friend, Jim; teachers past and present; and clients, friends and students on this all-important journey. Thank you.

To all elephants subjected to force and harm for the sake of human entertainment, may you be free from suffering.

Introduction

A Personal Journey

In the winter of 2013, my canine companion of fifteen years, Shyla, began her final exit. In those last few heartrending days, I alternated between tending to her rapidly declining body and praying and meditating by her side—holding sacred watch for her passage.

My intimate partner, Jim, held space with us both during this time as I embraced, fed, cleaned, and caressed her until her last breath. Only a few months in our new home I purchased with the intention of making her final *years* comfortable, her head and shoulders suddenly jerked upward as if being pulled by a strong force. Startled, my own breath stopped abruptly. She collapsed back to the floor. That dramatic breath was her last. Shyla, as I knew and loved her, was never to breathe again.

Our move to the cozy mountain home followed living remotely together for ten years in a single-room cabin with no indoor plumbing or running water. We lived what I came to know as a blessed life with all the freedoms afforded voluntary simplicity—no neighbors; clear, star-filled skies; an intimate connection with the land; and the wild animal community—coupled with access to modern technology. With a few solar panels and automotive batteries powering a cell phone, laptop, sparse lighting, and music I connected with the world.

After a winter of carrying all our water up the eighth-mile long path, I installed a roof catchment system and barrels, which, with rare exception, provided all the water needed for bathing and cleaning. A chainsaw and backpack enabled me to cut and pack enough wood (sometimes up to a quarter-mile through painstakingly steep hills) to keep us warm during the winter.

Daily living chores kept us both busy and in excellent shape, and yet there was still time to complete a bachelor's and master's degree at a university some seventy miles away, thanks to distance learning empowered by technology. I was also taking a path of recovery from codependence, adult children of alcoholics, alcohol and substance use after the end of a thirteen-year relationship. The time and space afforded me a rich period of growth, aliveness, and spiritual wonder. Shyla, a shepherd mix, was continually by my side adventuring, protecting, and nourishing me.

From the moment our breaths first connected—when as a pup, she lay shivering from fright on my chest—to the moment of her brusque final exhale, Shyla was my life partner and spiritual companion. Later, the profundity of being so consciously present during her dying days catapulted me on a then unknowable journey of inspired service—of which this book is a strand.

I cultivated some very simple but powerful tools that helped me through the most difficult and rewarding experience of my life. Shortly after, I wrote my first book about these tools and her transition experience. It revolved around creating what I call a *compassionate container* for our spiritual practice, but really, they are tools for life.

From that book *(Companioning the Sacred Journey: A Guide to Creating a Compassionate Container for Your Spiritual Practice, 2013)* arose courses based on three main tools—*journaling, compassion-based mindfulness, and conscious intentions*—and my career as a mindfulness teacher and mindfulness-based life coach launched.

This book arises out of the courses I've developed and taught and the coaching services I offer. It is an accumulation of insight, story, exercises, and practices since that fateful experience with Shyla some five years ago.

Living remotely as we did, I only enjoyed periodic contact with mindfulness teachers and other practitioners. I hadn't realized that the meditation method I practiced for the previous twenty years had become secularized and formalized in Western culture. I learned mindfulness as *Vipassana*, or *Insight Meditation*, and today it is known simply as *mindfulness*.

This practice is now embedded in over a thousand programs in hospitals, medical centers, and clinics throughout the United States alone. Additionally, it is taught in schools, corporations, the military, and even Wall Street. The subject and study is so pervasive, it's made the covers of *Time Magazine* and *Scientific American*. Articles are frequently seen in the *Wall Street Journal*, the *New York Times*, and *Forbes*. Simply put, it is extremely popular and very mainstream in America.

Combining *compassion-based mindfulness* practices with conscious intention creates an exciting catalyst to build a life of authentic meaning and value—one of inner peace, personal clarity, emotional freedom and joy. Basically, a life we can truly love.

As research into the powerful effects of mindfulness continues, I can better bring these tools to my clients and students, helping them to stop the pain associated with a variety of ailments, including stress, stress-related illnesses, and emotional reactivity. I can also help them grow their personal clarity, joy, and happiness.

Mindfulness, compassion, and intentioned living help us learn how to live wisely through the inevitable difficulties of life—as in losing a loved one, experiencing emotional turmoil, illness, or aging.

There are hundreds of books on learning mindfulness and compassion practices—some by researchers and clinicians, others that are simply warm and inspiring, and even some by masters in mindfulness' wisdom tradition, Buddhism. This book and the courses I teach offer mindfulness and compassion practices with a life-coaching approach. This empowers readers and students to gain not only the focus, clarity, emotional freedom, and inner ease that mindfulness and compassion practices foster but also a growing and engaged connection with profound self-knowledge and unique expression that creates a life grounded in authenticity, meaning and joy. A life that cultivates the emergence of the vibrant aliveness that is yearning to be lived through each of us in every moment.

Undertaking this work helps reconnect heart, mind, and body to better live an authentic values-based life filled with meaning and joy—a life we can love.

I specifically chose to emphasize the compassion component in my practice and teachings because of my personal history growing up in an abusive alcoholic home environment. This experience left me riddled with self-hatred and low self-esteem. I'm not alone in this. The American culture is dominated by it as we'll learn more about later.

When the roots of mindfulness are carefully studied, the practices are inseparable from compassion and loving-kindness. In the West, we have a tendency to disconnect our thinking mind from our heart space. I coined the term *compassion-based mindfulness* to ensure inclusiveness of these two aspects of our nature.

Mindfulness without heart and compassion may widen the gap that we, as individuals, cultures, and even as a species, so desperately need to close—our potential for happiness, joy, love, connection, and health. Reconnecting heart, mind, and body is critical to our happiness and fulfillment as human beings, the health of our body, and the vibrancy of our planet. I believe that this separation is at the core of the maladies of Western civilization and what is leading us to the utter decimation of the planet.

Regardless of the particular circumstances of our individual lives, we each have a great burden to bear. It is the inescapable nature of being a human being in a human body—a body that is born, experiences illness, loss, aging, and eventually death. Not that this is the sum of our experience, but until we learn to meet these fated experiences more wakefully and compassionately, we live in bondage to them— never at peace and never reaching more than momentary pleasure or contentment.

Meeting our human burden fully and mindfully, with a tender, open heart is a path that can lead to greater peace, clarity, emotional freedom, and joy. And when there is inner peace, there is a chance for outer peace.

Bangkok, Thailand
January 2018

Why Compassion-Based Mindfulness?

Love and compassion are necessities, not luxuries. Without them, humanity cannot survive.

— His Holiness, the Fourteenth Dalai Lama of Tibet

I recently gave a talk on mindfulness and stress reduction to a women's luncheon group at a Native American wellness center. I have been professionally and personally connected with members of the Pomo tribe in my hometown community for over twenty years. There's an unexplainable and deep sister like bond with one tribal spiritual leader, a petite, strong-willed woman in her late sixties.

About a year prior to this talk, her eighteen-year-old granddaughter committed suicide. When I attended the wake, I was deeply jolted—such a vibrant, capable, bright light in the community I watched grow through the years chose to end her life. I know it's a symptom of a bigger problem currently with youth in America—part of a vast and growing cultural side effect of our choice of values, I believe. When I see it in the tribal community, though, I'm even more affected.

It wasn't but a few years later another tribal member I'd known and taught since second grade ended his life too. I was so mad at this now new father that I cursed at him during the wake and the burial.

"Dammit! So intelligent and now your daughter grows up fatherless! Dammit!"

The ripple effects of horrific generational trauma and dysfunction persist in some Native American communities, despite the many efforts to transform it. Suicide amongst Native youth can be as much as ten times the national average.[1]

In between sobs at the wake of my friend's granddaughter, I shook my head and asked her, "What can we do?"

When I picked my friend up for the luncheon that day, her cousin, who also happened to be a grandmother of this young woman, joined us. I hadn't realized at the time, but during the lunch, I was seated next to the two grandmothers and the mother of this young woman who abruptly ended her life. As it turned out, the monthly luncheon was *started* in response to her granddaughter's suicide in an attempt to bring the women of our local tribal communities together.

How does one meet a tragedy such as our daughter, granddaughter, or son committing suicide? I was so overtaken by this question during my talk.

> *How could some scientific research and a few mindful exercises touch the pain and suffering born by just these three women, much less the whole native community?*

When I met the cultural specialist for the center before the event, he likened present-day mindfulness to the cultural tradition of basket weaving. Intention and focused attention are cultivated and paramount for the weavers. Our local Pomo tribes are world-renowned for their baskets. Since most cultural practices of Native Americans are usually conscious and prayerful action, I recognized within them the three main attributes of a mindfulness practice: attention, intention, and

---

[1] Horowitz, S. (2014, March 9). The hard lives — and high suicide rate — of Native American children on reservations. *Washington Post*.

attitude. As I relayed this information to the women during the talk, I could see my friend searching inwardly.

When I moved into why we add compassion to our mindfulness practice, I referenced the Buddhist understanding of the ten thousand joys and ten thousand sorrows that accompany a life in the body. Through nodding heads, I could see there was a deep understanding by everyone in the room.

Our local tribes were virtually extinguished, save a few families, in the genocidal efforts of early European settlers in Lake County, California. In one particularly gruesome incident, the Bloody Island Massacre, families survived by submerging themselves and their children under the water using a reed to keep oxygen flowing into their lungs while horrifying indiscriminate killing unfolded all around them.

Not one person from the tribe is free from the effects caused by these earlier gruesome experiences. Everyone has been affected by them, and the repercussions of these actions continue to ripple throughout both the tribal and nontribal community.

Just a brief reflection of our own lives may help us recognize how we are all vulnerable to suffering—no one is excluded. And while we most likely have not experienced tragedies of the magnitude of these women and their families, we all have suffering. It is part of being human.

I went on to explain how we can use compassion to help us meet all life's challenges—from illness, the aging body, the loss of loved ones, and, eventually, our own death. May we never be presented with harsh tragedies in our life, but at some point, while details differ, we can rest assured we all have our burdens to bear.

Burdens and challenges in life are inevitable, just as the sprout has to push its way through the skin of the seed.

During the firestorm of 2015 in my community, some twelve hundred plus homes were destroyed and four lives taken in a matter of hours. The stories of tragedy and loss from this one event—displacement, lost treasures, disrupted lives and goals, lost forests and wildlife—will reverberate for many generations to come. And while our instinct may be to say, "You're fortunate that more lives weren't lost," or "At least you had insurance," it is important to honor and tenderly receive the gamut of emotional reaction to a disaster if we are to find our way through to full healing.

It is this recognition—none of us escape painful sorrows in this life—that beckons us to meet our own and others' pain with compassion. Our natural instinct is to reach out and help those we see who are hurt or suffering. As we undertake a mindfulness practice, we also actively practice taking a compassionate approach to what we meet as we turn our gaze inward. We learn to meet all the pain and complexity of our lives with loving awareness.

We also learn not to take these difficulties personally, as if we're the only one experiencing them or that maybe we've done something wrong to create them, but rather to more fully see their nature as just part of the human experience—meeting them affectionately head on.

Compassion is a loving and kind way to meet pain
and suffering—our own and others.

To share one more story: Kisa, a young married woman in India during the time of the Buddha, lost her one-year-old son from a sudden illness. Out of desperation, she went from household to household, begging for a way to bring him back to life.

She came across a kind-faced woman who directed her to see the Buddha himself. The Buddha smiled compassionately and conveyed that there was only one way to solve her problem. "Bring me a few mustard seeds from a house that has not seen death."

With a spark of hope, Kisa spent the day scurrying from home to home in her village. "Please, please," she pleaded. "Can you help me?"

Even though each house had mustard seeds, each time, she left empty-handed. "I can give you the seeds," they replied, "but it would not fulfill the request."

Kisa heard many stories that day, some of graceful exits and some of tragic endings. As the day wore on, her tired feet dragged, her hope waned. As night fell and the first stars lifted their heads, a great learning had taken place for Kisa: Death is universal. Not a home in her village had escaped it. She sighed with grief and understanding. Further, she came to know that if the Buddha were to bring her son back, he would eventually die again.

Death is a part of life and none of us get out of our story alive.

The story of Kisa touches me because it speaks to the impersonal nature of pain and suffering itself. Ultimately, there isn't anything I can do to alter these facts of life—whether I'm a good person or bad, famous or infamous, chronically ill or healthy all my life—I, too, will someday reach my end and die. So if there is no way for us or anyone, really, to get around these experiences, how then can we take them personally? Equally, how can we not have compassion for ourselves and others?

Creating Our Container

Chapter 1

Components of a Compassionate Container

A compassionate container includes more than our surroundings—it includes the attention, attitude, and intention we bring to our lives.

Committing to a new journey of self-discovery can be an exciting adventure, and a great starting point is creating a safe and supportive "space" or "field"—what I call a *compassionate container*. This container "holds" us and our unfolding experience, carrying us into the next.

Since we are a heart, mind, and body moving through time and space, our *container* is fashioned out of more than just the physical space we find ourselves. Our *container* includes the *attention, attitude, and intention* we bring to any given moment. Each of these not only affects our own experience in the moment but also contributes to creating our future, affecting our relationships, and influencing others' experiences.

Here's a brief look at each.

Intention

*Intention is the purpose or aspiration we hold for
our forthcoming actions and experience.*

Intention is getting conscious about what we want to create for our experience and our lives. As part of our *container*, intention speaks to how we want to meet ourselves, others, and what happens.

For example, if I'm entering a situation where I will meet new people, I can set an intention to be as fully present, open, and loving as I can. Becoming conscious about that will affect my actions, how I receive and respond to people, and how people receive and respond to me. They may feel safer and more willing to share openly with me, which could lead to a loving and interesting exchange. Just aspiring to this—*making it conscious and intentional*—will change the experience; hence, it contributes to the *container* of those moments we share with others.

*Just to note: setting an intention doesn't guarantee
a situation will turn out as we intend, but it will
surely create a greater likelihood of it doing so.*

As you undertake the exercises and practices outlined in this book, I invite you to set an intention of creating a safe, kind, and compassionate *container* for yourself. If you are working with others through this material, I encourage you to intend a sense of safety and acceptance for all who are participating.

Since you can set an intention for anything, you may also want to consider setting an intention of openness and possibility for unforeseen magnificence. At the very least, setting an intention to befriend yourself on this journey can open many wondrous possibilities.

Exercise: Setting Intentions for This Work

The Mindful and Intentional Living courses are usually held in intimate small group settings. To help create a strong container for the course, students are asked to make a few commitments. Feel free to modify these if you are using the book as a personal guide or with a group on your own.

- Attend every session from beginning to end
- Arrive prepared and on time
- Commit to using direct communication
- Tell the truth as best you can
- Honor your body
- Stay current with the work
- Maintain confidentiality

To increase the chances of a greater synchronicity, flow, and transformation, everyone is invited to courageously undertake the intention of the following:

- Getting vulnerable
- Trusting your intuition
- Creating a tender net of support as you discover difficult things about yourself and life
- Being your word (keeping commitments) particularly to yourself
- Letting go of "right" and "wrong" or "black and white" thinking
- Being gentle with yourself
- Keeping the focus on yourself and your own process by not offering well-intentioned but unasked for advice to others

- Being willing to take risks—leaning into places of resistance and fear and "jumping over the fence"
- Taking full responsibility for your engagement with the material (any and all benefit received from the work is directly related to your level of commitment and participation with the materials, exercises, and practices)

Attitude

> *Look out, everyone! I'm going to be crabby for the rest of the day!*
>
> *—Lucy Van Pelt, Peanuts comic strip character*

Remember Lucy from *Peanuts*? She was notoriously critical of Charlie Brown and over the moon attracted to Schroeder. Her *attitude—her way of thinking or feeling about*—Charlie Brown set the stage for her actions toward him. How many times did she pull the football away from "good ole" trusting Charlie Brown? Her attitude toward Schroeder oscillated between fawning and frustration. Each attitude Lucy held created a different set of circumstances and reactions.

The attitude we choose in any given moment not only colors our experience and actions in response to what is happening but also deeply affects others. I recently had an exchange with a woman who was angry at me for turning her in for smoking in a nonsmoking hotel. Never mind that it was my partner who mentioned it to the management. She took it upon herself to approach me one morning during breakfast.

Her sudden anger really threw me off guard as she accosted me on the way to our room. I had no clue who this small terse woman was, and you can bet that her tight and angry attitude toward me had a powerful impact on my reaction to her and, unfortunately, the rest of my morning activities!

Attitude is a choice.

As hard as it is sometimes to choose it—in the instance above, I tried my best to take an attitude of kindly moving toward a solution but was overtaken by triggered trauma response and turned and walked away—attitude is a choice.

Attitudes contribute to our overall health and well-being and, as we'll discover later, contribute to whether this moment is joyful and playful or stressful, hurtful, or painful.

Of the three factors, attitude and intention set the tone of the moment.

The invitation as we undertake a mindfulness practice is to cultivate an attitude of kind curiosity to receive each moment; to create an open and loving field to receive life as it unfolds.

We practice this by engaging with the part of our self that honestly doesn't know what is going to happen in any given moment because in the deepest sense of truth, this or any moment in the future has never happened before. And while we can make assumptions based on strong correlation and tendencies about what will most likely occur or expectations about what we'd like to see happen, the truth is we really don't know with absolute certainty. Therefore, adopting an attitude of open curiosity is really an honest and authentic way to approach any moment.

Piqued interest has a tendency to create unique conditions, adding a freshness to any situation. Any time we purposefully adopt an attitude of open discovery, our attachment to the outcome almost magically disappears and is replaced with a wondrous delight to see what actually unfolds. There is more spaciousness to experience the mysterious dance of life in the moment.

Attention

The difference between something good
and something great is attention to detail.

– Charles R. Swindoll

Another essential factor contributing to our *container* of any given moment is the quality of our *attention*, the mental faculty of considering or taking notice of someone or something. If our attention is divided, it means we aren't experiencing the current moment as fully as we can. Since the only time we can experience a moment is when it is happening, if our attention is scattered, we miss the only chance we have for that experience—ever.

Ever.

Bringing the fullest attention to the moment we have, on the other hand, means that we get the extremely precious gift of experiencing the richness and complexity of our sacred once-in-a-lifetime human experience.

Bringing our full attention to the moment
heightens awareness of all our sensory knowing,
sharpens clarity, and reveals previously unknown
layers of exquisite complexity and subtle pleasure.

One of the immediate benefits of a mindfulness practice is our increased attention to and awareness of the moment. As we begin, we are most likely experiencing only a mere fraction of what's available to us. Bringing our full attention to the moment heightens awareness of all our sensory knowing, sharpens clarity, and can reveal previously unexperienced layers of intricate complexity and subtle pleasure.

This aspect of our experience expands and deepens over time with practice. Since we can never *somatically* (experience in the body) know what we don't know until we actually viscerally touch it in the moment, we have but a rare chance to get near the totality of this uniquely magnificent, sublime moment without purposefully attending to our attention.

Fortunately, these three facets of our *container*—intention, attitude, and attention—are within our range of influence. They are vitally important in creating a lusciously rich and joyful life filled with value, meaning, and happiness. Using them is a way of creating a loving and caring environment for our mindfulness practice and life in general.

Chapter 2

Journaling as Companion

Journaling is any method that captures the spirit or essence of our experience in a valuable and meaningful way.

Another powerfully important piece of our *container* is journaling. A journal is a protected place to hold our inner experiences. Journaling as a practice establishes an authentic and meaningful relationship with ourselves—truly the most important relationship of our lives as we are our longest standing companion.

Undertaking journaling as a tool of self-discovery offers the opportunity—maybe for the first time in our lives—of intentionally listening to our inner self for understanding and meaning. Similarly, it can advance a wise, tender, trusting, and compassionate attitude.

If we have not journaled before, we will most likely be surprised with what is revealed through a practice.

Meeting ourselves with a gentle, curious, and kindhearted ear will carry us much further than

*an unforgiving harshness as we unearth the layers
of our uniqueness and further befriend ourselves.*

A journal provides a perfect vessel to glean wisdom; explore opinions, values, and passions; and work through difficult issues in a caring, confidential space.

In these enormously important ways, a journal can be an irreplaceable, constant, and, most importantly, nonjudgmental companion for our life's journey. Not that we won't see our own and others' judgments come through our journaling, but the source of those judgments will not be the journal itself.

In this way, our journal becomes a very rare and precious companion that is most always available and never critical of our path. This means we will never have to fear its capacity to hold it all or never be concerned it will run away. Its continual, steady presence is unequaled, and in that way, it also becomes a teacher, exampling how we can be more accepting of the gamut of our experiences, decisions, emotions, and expressions.

On top of that, a journal can be used as part of a *cradle of creation*, uncovering previously unexplored passions, or a place to discover new resources for our vitality and aliveness, maybe becoming a birthing place to expressing ourselves in more compelling, meaningful, and fulfilling ways.

One way to begin the discovery of who we are is through a simple inquiry that invites us to view ourselves in possibly a new light.

Exercise: If You Really Knew Me, You'd Know That . . .

This exercise may challenge some long-held beliefs around speaking confidently about ourselves, but you are encouraged to be as honest and forthcoming as possible.

> Set a timer for five minutes. Complete the following statement:
>
> "If you really knew me, you'd know that . . ."
>
> List as many positive and wonderful things that come to you. As you do, notice how you feel in your body. Is it uncomfortable? If so, where? Does it feel pleasant? Where do you notice that?
>
> When it seems you can't think of any more, try to remember a time when someone gave you a compliment. What were they pointing out? Can you receive it as true? If so, list it. If not, can you open to the possibility that it may be true? How does that feel in the body?
>
> After five minutes, take note—Was it difficult? Easy? How would it feel if you were invited to say it out loud to others? Journal about your experience of the exercise.

A significantly valuable use of a journal is to work through difficult issues and situations. When I'm struggling with emotions or getting caught in a complex situation, not knowing the best course of action, journaling helps me discover my honest thoughts and feelings about a situation, particularly when it's difficult to discern them. I can usually feel in my body when something isn't quite right, and journaling can help me get to the bottom of it.

Journaling is like talking to a trusted friend, opening a spacious field for revealing and purging inner turmoil, one where solace and comfort for any dilemma and distress can be found.

It also helps when I'm feeling stuck and can't quite pinpoint what's holding me back and what I need to do next. It has a tendency to make my subjective experiences and subconscious thoughts more available and tangible so I can see the situation more clearly.

Journaling also has a way of releasing the pent-up tension and pain associated with these troublesome situations. I find it much easier to work through issues with a journal, writing as if sharing with a reliable confidant. Something palpably shifts as jumbled thoughts tumble their sometimes messy way to paper.

The process somehow makes seemingly insurmountable problems more simple and manageable. Calmness and clarity arise from the very act of journaling. Something extremely cathartic takes place—a cleansing process of sorts that moves energy through in a way that frees up the mind for greater possibilities and choices.

> *Isn't it mysterious to begin a new journal like this? I can run my fingers through the fresh clean pages but I cannot guess what the writing on them will be.*
>
> —*Maud Hart Lovelace, Betsy in Spite of Herself*

What's exciting about journaling is it doesn't need to be solely composed of written words. Since journaling can be any means that has meaning for us, we can explore numerous ways to capture and process our experiences including drawing, voice recording, collaging, and collecting.

Computers and the electronic world have expanded our options for chronicling our lives. Now our Facebook page becomes a journal of ideas and events we wish to share with friends, family, and the larger community. As well, cameras and computers hold thousands upon thousands of images that reflect our experience, perspective, and play.

Even our body, whether knowingly or unknowingly, acts as a journal and reflection of our life experiences. From what we eat to how we dress and adorn it with makeup, tattoos, piercings, and the like, the body is an intimate expression of our lives to the extent that we can influence its expression as we are, of course, bound by certain limitations of the body we were born into.

As we use journaling as part of our *container*, we are not limited or committed to one kind. We can use multiple journals to meet our needs for different experiences and situations. The options are endless for what can become a meaningful journal for our travels through life.

I have a collection of heart rocks that serves as a journal of my travels. Even though today I wouldn't be able to tell you where and when I found most of them, this "journal" documents the joy I experience in my travels and, particularly, the joy of seeing a heart shape in nature.

Some like creating very special and sacred journals, keeping them formally secure. To the other extreme, I have friends who just use scraps of paper and burn or toss them away when they've finished writing or they've served their purpose. Writing in the sand, stacking rocks, arranging sticks, dancing to music or not—the creative options for journaling go on and on.

I provided crisis counseling to those suffering losses during the Valley Fire of 2015 in Lake County, California. It was heart-rending to learn from the survivors who lost their home and all belongings that the loss of their journals was one of the most difficult to bear.

Collecting keepsakes in a scrapbook or otherwise is another way to journal. I make a point of purchasing bookmarks, refrigerator magnets, and postcards on my travels to help remind me of the places I've been. I even collect fallen Bodhi tree leaves from special temples and use them as bookmarks. This growing collection of trinkets remind me how special and meaningful travel is for me.

> *Journals are a sacred companion to the preciousness*
> *that is our life.*

A journal can be used for directed writing exercises and inquiries, such as the one above, or as a space for free writing. There are journals designed with writing prompts that pique our curiosity and encourage discovery and others as simple as a sketch pad for drawings, coloring, and collages.

Julie Cameron, author of *The Artist's Way Morning Pages*, advocates a simple but potent exercise consisting of three pages of longhand, stream of consciousness writing, ideally done first thing in the morning. This process helps clear the mind, tune into ideas, and release anxiety.

Writing about traumatic, stressful, or emotional events results in improvements in both physical and psychological health. This form of writing, termed *expressive writing*, has demonstrated many health benefits over time according to a study in 2005,[2] including the following:

- Fewer stress-related visits to the doctor
- Improved immune system functioning
- Reduced blood pressure
- Improved lung and liver function
- Fewer days in hospital
- Improved mood
- Feeling of greater psychological well-being
- Reduced depressive symptoms before examinations
- Fewer posttraumatic intrusion and avoidance symptoms

In addition, these other outcomes have been reported.

- Reduced absenteeism from work
- Quicker reemployment after job loss
- Improved working memory
- Improved sporting performance
- Higher grade point average
- Altered social and linguistic behavior

It's important to point out that while most participants in the study references showed improvement in these areas, the author noted that expressive writing could be detrimental to adult survivors of childhood

---

[2] Baikie, K. A., & Wilhelm, K. (2005). Emotional and physical health benefits of expressive writing. *Advances in Psychiatric Treatment, 11*(5), 338–346. http://doi.org/10.1192/apt.11.5.338

abuse and for a small sample of Vietnam veterans with posttraumatic stress disorder (PTSD). *If you have experienced intense forms of trauma, I would strongly recommend working directly with a qualified therapist before considering this form of journaling.*

In essence, journaling becomes part of a *container of compassion* as we embark on a journey of self-discovery and a loving companion as we turn inward for the answers to our life questions. It is a simple, robust process that adds a sense of safety, wonder, and revelation to our sacred journey, and it helps us discover or rediscover core values, hopes, and dreams.

> *These empty pages are your future, soon to become your past. They will read the most personal tale you shall ever find in a book.*
>
> *—Anonymous*

When we wake up to the life that is here, we will not find a more amazing or remarkable story than our own.

Exercise: If I Really Knew Myself, I'd Know That . . .

Explore one or more of the following inquires using any type of journal that moves you:

- Reflect on what brought you to pick up this book (or take the course). What is it about your life at this time that calls you to this?
- What do you hope to get out of reading the book (or taking the course)?
- What concerns, if any, do you have in your life right now?

- What about this time of year or season are you grateful for?

By setting aside the time for inner inquiry and becoming conscious of the unconscious, journaling provides a vital tool for our self-discovery. It becomes an essential part of our compassionate container.

These indispensable pieces of our container—attitude, attention, intention, and journaling—prepare us for exploring and learning how to live a more mindful, meaningful, and joyful life.

Mindful Living

Chapter 3

What Is Mindfulness?

*I define mindfulness as the practice of being
fully present and alive, body and mind united.*

— *Ven. Thich Nhat Hanh*

Mindfulness is ubiquitous in America. There is rarely a person who hasn't heard of it. A Google search for mindfulness returns over thirty-nine million results. But just what is mindfulness?

The term *mindfulness* derives from the Pali word *sati,* which signifies presence of mind or attentiveness to the present. It is sometimes referred to as remembering or recollecting, and its history dates back some 2,500 years to the Theravada Buddhist tradition with the practices known as *Vipassana* or *Insight Meditation.*

Virtually every wisdom tradition has some form of mindfulness practice at its core as a way of stilling the body, mind, and heart to become aware of the sacred essence of the present. From indigenous peoples practicing conscious awareness to contemplative traditions, such as Jewish, Christian, and Islamic practices promoting stillness as a means to hear the word of God, some form of mindfulness has been pursued for millennia.

Only recently has mindfulness been secularized and formalized enough in Western and scientific culture to be considered a quality of human consciousness that can be measured and studied empirically. Though there isn't full consensus in the fields that study mindfulness, it can be seen as both a *process* (mindfulness practice) and an *outcome* (mindful awareness). So mindfulness is both a *practice* and a *way of being*.

Mindfulness is a way of perceiving that is not *thinking about* or *conceptualizing* but rather *knowing through direct experience*. It is sometimes referred to as *awareness*, *purposeful attention*, and *self-recollection*. The latter one helps me think we are *re-collecting* ourselves and our awareness to the present moment. We are aligning our heart, mind, and body with the present to experience it more fully.

Jon Kabat-Zinn, PhD, professor of medicine emeritus at the University of Massachusetts's medical school, defines mindful awareness as "the awareness that arises by paying attention on purpose, in the present moment, and nonjudgmentally." In 1979, he founded the Stress Reduction Clinic and the Center for Mindfulness in Medicine, Health Care, and Society, one of the first centers for mindfulness research.

Similarly, Diana Winston of UCLA's Mindfulness Research Center defines mindfulness as "paying attention to present moment experience with open curiosity and a willingness to be with what is."

I appreciate the definition by Paul Grossman, research director emeritus, department of psychosomatic medicine, division of internal medicine at the University Hospital, Basel, Switzerland: "Mindfulness may be seen as a form of naturalistic observation, or more precisely participant-observation, in which the objects of observation are the perceptible mental phenomena that arise during all states of waking consciousness."[3] This helps me understand that in addition

---

[3]   Grossman P. Mindfulness practice: A unique clinical intervention for the behavioral sciences. Self-improvement. Mindfulness. (n.d.). Retrieved February 23, 2018, from https://www.scribd.com/document/78210023/Paul-Grossman-Mindfulness-Practice-A-Unique-Clinical-Intervention-for-the-Behavioral-Sciences

to experiencing the moment directly, we are noticing what we are experiencing as we experience it; we are aware that we're aware as we are aware.

> *Mindfulness is our ability to be aware of what is going on both inside us and around us. It is the continuous awareness of our bodies, emotions, and thoughts.*

> *—Ven. Thich Nhat Hanh*

This simple definition of Thich Nhat Hanh, a famous and well-loved Buddhist monk from Vietnam, captures it well. This is the active collection of and connection between our hearts, minds, and bodies. We are both in our full experience and aware we are in it.

Mindfulness as a practice and just like our *container*, includes our attention, attitude, and intention. Remembering each of these is largely under our influence, we can choose to pay attention with the best quality of attention we have in any moment. We can choose our attitude, be it resistance, acceptance, judgment, allowance, or countless others. And we can set an intention to allow and receive all that arises.

So while the basis of mindfulness is awareness, the practice of mindfulness can be seen as:

> *Purposefully paying nonjudgmental attention to our present moment experience with an attitude of kind curiosity and an intention of acceptance and allowance.*

Since the purpose of learning mindfulness is to incorporate it into all areas of our lives, there are four *postures* used for formal practice—seated, standing, moving, and supine. But really, the purpose of the practices is to strengthen our mindful awareness in all areas, or postures, of living.

Stillness practices are sometimes referred to as meditation, and *movement practices* can include walking, yoga, qigong, and other slow, gentle forms of movement where we can cultivate deepened awareness of our experience.

The systematic practices can center on increasing awareness and focus and steadying our attention, while still others cultivate a quality of spaciousness and openness, creating a large *field* of awareness where allowance is fostered so experiences can arise and pass away without response. Supportive mindfulness practices include generating a particular type of experience, such as kindness, forgiveness, or stillness in the face of difficulty.

Everyone has the capacity for mindfulness. No one of us is without it. Here's a quick exercise to help you understand this capacity.

Exercise: One Unmindful Minute

Set a timer for sixty seconds, and for that duration, try NOT to be aware of anything—sound, sight, sensation, etc.

What did you notice? Were you able to NOT feel, think, hear, see anything? Where was your attention? In your body? On your thoughts? Thinking what a crazy exercise this is?

We all are aware of something, but the question is, of what? It is not uncommon today to have the vast majority of our attention focused in our thinking world. When asked what the purpose of the body was, a young second grader answered matter-of-factly, "to hold our head." We live in our minds. Whether judging, planning, fantasizing or sometimes just spacing out, it's how we spend a lot of our time.

Mindfulness of the present is something that everyone has the capability of strengthening. Attention and focus practices increase our capacity to experience things in fuller and more vivid richness. Gathering our attention to our present experience increases the lucidity of that experience, enlivening our conscious connection to the only place and time we can experience the goodness that is available to us— this place at this time.

If we wish to experience the great depths of joy and happiness that are available to us as human beings, we will need to open to the full gamut of experience—pain and sorrow, joy and love.

Shutting out part of our experience dampens our capacity to experience all parts.

As counterintuitive as this may sound, we may think by not feeling the difficult, and only opening for the good, we can bypass experiencing pain and suffering. It is, unfortunately, a truth and reality that most of us who practice mindfulness come to realize. We must experience it all if we are to live to our fullest capacity of aliveness and joy.

While we can practice paying more attention to the good experiences as a way of growing our happiness, which will be explored later, avoiding or resisting any direct experience creates pain and suffering in itself as does chasing after pleasant experiences.

If directly meeting and accepting the more challenging situations in our lives is key in mindfulness practice, it becomes quite easy to see why adopting an attitude of kindness and compassion becomes an important component of our practice. Painful situations, which we all experience at some point in life, can be difficult enough to face. Encouraging an attitude of kindness and acceptance, which can help us move through these inevitable situations more smoothly, becomes a loving and wise approach.

There is a dynamic, blissful experience and wiser, expansive knowing waiting for us on the other side of a mindfulness practice. Listening carefully to our unique life as it unfolds with a reverence and curiosity begins this journey, and a consistent, steady practice leads to it, lifting any moment to a more subtle, sumptuous experience.

Mindfulness, as Tara Brach shares, is a way of *listening to our lives*. For me, it is a way of listening deep enough so I can align and harmonize my heart, mind, and body for my greatest good.

Chapter 4

Compassion-Based Mindfulness

Compassion involves recognizing our shared human condition, flawed and fragile as it is.

—Dr. Kristin Neff

Compassion is sometimes seen as "suffering with," but that is more like *empathy*—the ability to understand and share another's feelings. I see compassion more as understanding another's feelings and experience enough to be moved to want to help relieve suffering when we see it. This is also how researchers dealing with emotions distinguish it.

We instinctively want to sooth another's pain. Just notice how you feel when a baby cries or when you see an injured animal or someone you love in pain.

Our brains are actually wired to respond with nurturing when we see suffering or distress.

Engaging in a mindfulness practice will, over time, strengthen this instinctive nurturing part of ourselves, and if a compassionate attitude is purposefully cultivated, it will deepen it even further.

> *By purposefully combining compassion and mindfulness, we actively develop and elevate the goodness in our heart.*

But if meeting suffering with compassion is our natural tendency, why is there so much callousness in the world? Why do we sometimes see someone suffering and turn away, quickly moving on? What gets in our way?

Research indicates that when it comes to showing compassion to others, being in a hurry may actually prevent us from reaching out to help. Access to the compassionate part of ourselves seems to deaden in the face of hurried life. Our increasingly fast-paced culture requires us to operate at quicker speeds all the time and that could be contributing to a less caring and sensitive population.

I've noticed when traveling, particularly in Asia, people pay much more attention and concern to not only helping when there is a challenging situation but also taking the time and attention to prevent difficult circumstances. Particularly, driving in Thailand may seem disorderly and chaotic, but upon careful study, the attitude seems to be one of wanting to make sure everyone makes it to their destination safely.

When it comes to *self-compassion*, in addition to a hurried lifestyle, other things—such as our perceived sense of value or worth—can get in the way, making self-compassion elusive. We may have learned through our family or societal systems to "buck up and take it" or, in my case personally, to "quit your crying or I'll give you something to cry about."

If you're a woman, you may also have learned that "you're *too* emotional" or there was no room for emotions at all. Each of these lends itself to the disconnection of the heart and mind from the body, which has detrimental impacts to our life satisfaction.

I remember when in my late twenties, my mother died suddenly of an aneurism. Within moments, she was brain dead, and in less than twenty-four hours, she was gone. When the doctor gave the family the news that she was brain dead and we had a choice to keep her on life support or not, the shock caused an immediate flooding of uncontrollable tears. I ran out of the conference room and locked myself in the bathroom. Within minutes, my aunt knocked and spoke through the locked door, "Now come on, Jody (my pet name), you must be strong." I took this to mean to stop crying.

Within the week, my partner was echoing a similar sentiment. When I had to step out in uncontrollable tears during the first family dinner at my mom's house after her death, he followed me and asked, "Are you sure you're not just doing this for attention?"

Being naive with exploring, owning, and honoring my emotions, I questioned my motivation for the tears that evening. At that time, I trusted others' opinions of my experience over my own. With a similar attitude, I've stifled some of the most intense and important emotional experiences of my life. I've come to learn that this is one of the most damaging and unnecessary approaches to human emotions as it stifles our instinctual loving responsiveness to suffering. It suppresses a kind and helpful response not only toward ourselves but also to our families, friends, loved ones, and, eventually, our communities. It also stifles one of our most important internal guides to life available to us.

It wasn't until my partner's father suddenly passed away some years later that he apologized for his insensitivity to my experience with my mom's death. This speaks not only to his own growing understanding of love for his father and emotional space but also to the difference of knowing something conceptually versus from direct experience.

Creating a container of compassion for these intense and heartfelt experiences is not only critical in ensuring we are present for the most important moments of our lives but also one of the essential elements for any sense of freedom and happiness in life.

Self-Compassion and Mindfulness

Through compassion-based mindfulness, we actively cultivate a compassionate response to ourselves and others.

Dr. Kristin Neff, associate professor of human development and culture in the educational psychology department at University of Texas at Austin and author of *Self Compassion: The Proven Power of Being Kind to Yourself*, sees self-compassion as the emotional heart of mindfulness, and I tend to agree.

Emotions are our innate guiding force that help us define our values and our sense of who we are and alerts us to when we are acting out of alignment with these. If we cultivate situations and conditions where emotions are not allowed to surface fully and freely and where we can't use them as a guiding light, then not only will we get off track and find ourselves doing things against our own health, values, logic and heart, but we will also lose the opportunity to experience the full richness available to us that can only be experienced through our emotional body. And if we shut down the experience of our emotions, we certainly won't know how to compassionately meet ourselves.

Touching our feelings directly gives us the best opportunity for loving self-care and a wise response to life's challenges. This requires a sense of safety within our lives and with ourselves.

In my early years, I learned how to stifle my feelings using anything and everything I could—substances, sex, shopping, gambling, food— you name it. I did everything I could to not experience the confusing pain of growing up around chaotic addictive dysfunction.

Unfortunately, covering over my feelings created a painfully inauthentic life of continually running from all emotions—particularly those trying to sound the alarm of living unaligned with my values. I ended up living lies upon lies with even more lies to cover up all the lies! It was a very painful period that resulted in heartbreaking and agonizing low self-esteem. I honestly felt wholly undeserving of living and unworthy of love.

It didn't come to an end until I entered recovery and did the work around being an adult child of an alcoholic. It was through this work I learned that not only were my emotions all right to feel but they were also the flagship of my values and accurately pointed to an unhealthy family system filled with crazy-making behaviors.

Today my emotions are not only an indicator of living life within the value system that resonates deep within my heart but also what makes my inner emotional life so rich and fulfilling. And I would have never been able to fully face the unfinished business of my past if it weren't for taking a compassionate stance toward myself and, eventually, my family.

Taking an attitude of compassion and kindness toward ourselves is paramount in healing the harms of the past, but it is equally important for the everyday wounds of life too.

> *Self-compassion is as natural and effective as an animal licking their wounds when injured. A healing salve is offered through our own kind attention.*

Taking the time to nurture and care for ourselves during difficult times helps keeps us healthy, balanced, and whole.

Sometimes our cultural and familial conditioning is so deep and wounding that our capacity to open up and build self-compassion is difficult and slow. But as a friend in recovery once commented, "At least I've stopped digging the hole!" Just undertaking the intention and practices of self-compassion ends the downward spiral of suffering and puts us instead on a path to healing and wholeness.

Remembering we can meet and respond to our experiences with any attitude we choose, choosing to meet ourselves and our suffering with compassion is not only a wise response but also the response that can lead to the most peace, freedom, and happiness. With compassion-based mindfulness practices, we actively reinforce and grow our natural capacity for self-compassion. Mindfulness and compassion practices go hand in hand not only because of the acquired wisdom of a two-thousand-five-hundred-year-old tradition or even because emerging scientific research points to it but also because our direct experience confirms it. The practices lead to a directly felt sense and deeper understanding of all that it is to be human in relationship with ourselves, other living beings, our communities and cultures, and the world at large.

There is no better time and place than the present to get started with this discovery for yourself.

Chapter 5

Collecting Our Attention

Where is the only time and place we can experience happiness?

Now.
Here.
Now. Here.
Now-here.
Nowhere.

All the evidence in the world means very little to our *own* happiness if we don't actually engage in the practices that lead to this happiness. The felt sense of a compassionate stance toward ourselves or the subtleties and nuances of states of bliss can never be fully conveyed through concepts and words.

Conceptualizing is one way of knowing; we can form an idea about something. But experience

is completely different; we engage in practical
contact, the felt sense of experience.

No matter how many research studies are conducted or experts tell us about the rewards of a mindfulness or compassion practice, until we open to the enriching experience available through actually applying the techniques to our own lives, it is all uncertain. We can't experience happiness by thinking or talking about it—by conceptualizing about it—we must fully engage with our experience to truly know happiness. In fact, when your attention is on thinking about happiness, you'll miss out on the sumptuous richness of the experience itself.

Thinking about happiness can actually keep you
from experiencing happiness.

When I first heard the question, "*Where* do we experience happiness?" I was stumped. I'd never really thought about it before. I was busy trying to *attain* happiness as I assumed was everyone else. I considered it some type of lifetime goal, some *place* to reach.

I have, like so many others of my generation in the United States, aspired for and lived our present-day prescription for happiness—a wealthy lifestyle filled with opulent beauty, attendance at well-to-do events, a perfect relationship with the perfect person, etc. But no one ever asked *where* I would experience this happiness once I *had* it. I was pretty sure, though, I knew *how* to get happiness.

It didn't become readily apparent to me until, having practiced mindfulness long enough, a deep awareness of connection between physical sensations and emotional experiences was drawn. Only then did it become obvious—the only place we can *experience* happiness is *in our bodies* through our sense doors—the eyes, ears, nose, mouth, and sensation. It's the only place we experience anything.

I never thought about *when* either as happiness was always something I was headed toward. Oh, there were fleeting moments of what I thought was happiness, but I always quickly headed to the next happiness "hit."

Yet as I began hearing from my teachers, happiness in the past is but a memory, and happiness in the future is just a fantasy—memory, a reflection; fantasy, a projection.

> *Only here, now, can happiness—or any experience—really be touched.*

So, as sense would have it, if I *really* want happiness, joy, or any emotional encounter, I will need to be aware of what happens as it happens; I need to be *here*, *now* as best I can.

Mindfulness increases our focus and heightens awareness of an experience as it happens. Over time, the practice illuminates and increases our conscious contact with the moment. What's hard to understand when we first start practicing is that we aren't fully experiencing the moment as completely as possible. *We can't recognize what we aren't experiencing because we aren't experiencing it. We can't know what we don't know.*

This is why committing to practice, even when what we're looking for isn't evident, is vital to our success.

> *In the beginning, it is a practice of faith. We are relying on concepts, guidance, and pointers from our teachers.*

In a short time of diligent practice, we, too, will experience the known benefits.

This reminds me of another story in the Buddhist tradition. At a monastery in Thailand where part of the mission was to translate the teachings of the sacred texts, a newly arrived monk, Teo, was assigned to help. He quickly noticed that the other monks were copying from already translated copies rather than from the original works.

When he inquired to the elderly abbot, Pua Tom, the abbot first responded with certitude, "Yes, we copy from the copies as we have for generations. The original texts are held in the center of the main *stupa*."

(A *stupa* is a structure at a monastery that usually holds some relic of the Buddha or other important monk or nun.)

"But," Teo inquired respectfully, "by copying the copies, if there is an error, that error continues on indefinitely."

Pua Tom responded thoughtfully, "I can see your concern. Yes, it would make better sense to copy from the originals. I will look into this."

Pua Tom left Teo's company, and as the afternoon wore on and Pua Tom hadn't resurfaced, Teo went down to the stupa. Seeing the abbot's inward footsteps in the dust but not seeing them return out, Teo entered the cavernous hallway.

As he got closer to the center, he could hear a drumlike sound stifled by the dank interior walls of the stupa. Each step brought a new sound—drumming turned to human grunting and, eventually, wailing.

Entering, Teo, saw Pua Tom hitting his head against the thick wall and, hearing his moanful wailing, called out, "Abbot! Abbot! What is the matter?"

The abbot, oblivious at first to Teo's presence, jerked awake and, with tears of frustration, called out, "The word was 'celebrate'! CELEBRATE!"

And so the importance of seeing for ourselves—of not taking anyone's word but our own—becomes critical to practicing mindfulness. We can give indications of the experience, but nothing can equal the direct experience.

*   *   *

As we turn our attention to various aspects of our experience—sights, sounds, sensations, smells, and tastes—we discover a whole new world available to us as never before, except perhaps in our early childhood years of wondrous discovery. Some see mindfulness as a return to this newness, and living mindfully is often referred to as living from a "*beginner's mind*." Logically, since we haven't yet experienced this particular moment and all that it holds, it is new—new to our senses and, when we are consciously aware of it, new to our heart and mind.

Interestingly enough and contrary to what we may believe, research points to turning our conscious attention to moment by moment experience as a means to reach greater contentment and happiness. But without some training, our attention seems to just wander endlessly. It is commonly likened to an unruly monkey wreaking havoc in the forest—first here, then there, then off to nowhere with no real steadiness. This scattered attention makes our experience of this moment ephemeral at best and painful at worst—the pain arising from the disconnection of our hearts, minds, and bodies from full experience and the divine mystery.

How are we to reach the happiness that lies within?

I remember vividly the dismal experience in my early twenties when I first tried to meditate. I set up a cushion against the wall in my brightly lit upstairs bedroom. A soft breeze fluttered the curtains, revealing sounds and smells of early spring.

I closed my eyes and, immediately, was clobbered with harsh judgmental thoughts and anxious fidgeting. In less than thirty seconds, I bounced off my cushion as if my skin were crawling with some unimaginable creepy bug. The moments following included a huge sense of failure and disappointment.

I couldn't stop my thoughts. And wasn't that the point of meditation? I was so trapped in my mind, I couldn't even recognize that I was *having* thoughts. I was just *believing* and *wrestling* with them. "There must be something wrong with me. I can't stop my thoughts for even one second."

A few years later, in desperation over an illness and troubles in my intimate relationship, I happened upon a ten-day silent meditation retreat in the mindfulness tradition. It was here, for the first time, I was able to experience my thoughts in a new way.

The shift begins by learning how to collect our attention through focusing the mind on a simple object—such as a sound, an item of interest, or the breath. Each has the potential to anchor our attention to the present moment.

When practiced over time, this develops our ability to steady and maintain focus for longer periods and how to return again and again to the present moment after our mind wanders, as it will often do.

It is common when starting a mindfulness practice to begin with the breath as a primary object of focus. There are many benefits to this as the breath is the following:

- Always with us - Everywhere we go, everything we do, the breath is naturally with us.
- Self-generating - Unlike a sound or an image we produce, the mind receives a rest from actively *creating or controlling* and takes on a new role of *observing*.
- Always changing - While breaths can be similar, no breath is like any other. Recognizing its uniqueness brings a quality of new aliveness to each inhale and exhale. With the breath, we witness directly the ever-changing nature of reality.
- Going nowhere - And yet the cycle of the breath is continuous, so we needn't concern ourselves with where it goes or that it may end.
- Mostly neutral - Unless we have issues that make breathing difficult, the body breathes itself effortlessly and without strain or pain. (In fact, breathing can bring much pleasantness to our experience, which will be explored later.)
- Body-based - Rather than a thought-based focal point, which keeps us anchored in the thinking mind, attention to the body brings us more fully into our direct experience engaged in the senses. We shift from conceptual knowing to experiential knowing. We learn how to embody our heart, mind, and body through the breath.

One of the defining characteristics of mindfulness is shifting the attention and focus of the mind from creation and judgment to observation, discovery, allowance, and experience. Taking a curious attention to the breath disengages us from our stories of the past and future and opens up an opportunity of knowing in the *somatic*, or body-based, field of experience.

The breath is something to befriend on the journey of life as it is immediately responsive to the needs of the body—a self-regulating system that can bring peace, clarity, and openness not only to our bodies but also to our hearts and minds. As Ryan Eliason, a transformational business coach, offers, change the state of just one aspect of being (mind, emotions, or body) and you change all three. So we begin.

Exercise: Building a Supportive Container for Practice

Because our intention is to build a stable and consistent practice, we'll spend time attending to creating an inviting container. The container will evolve over time as you are encouraged to modify it as your practice and loving relationship with yourself grows and deepens.

Begin by finding a place of quiet—one where you can rest undisturbed for brief to longer periods. If you can, keep the space free of mechanical noises (clocks, fans, etc.) and, optimally, near a window or door that can connect you to natural sounds and lighting. (During fair weather, you may want to create a pleasant outdoor space for practice.)

Create a space that evokes a feeling of reverence, pleasantness, comfort, and ease through placing attractive, soothing objects. You can light a candle in the space when you enter or place a simple bowl of water on a colored cloth, but try not to add anything too distractive. Simple is usually better.

It is helpful to use a timer with a soft sound that won't jar you when the session ends. There are helpful timer applications, such as Insight Meditation Timer, that are specific for meditation. Some even connect you to a community of meditators.

Include a chair and cushions in the space and feel free to alternate between them as needed. Shifting to gain comfort during the beginning of a session and again if discomfort arises is perfectly natural, particularly as you first start to practice. I find it helpful to alternate postures—sitting in a chair one time, a cushion on my bottom the next, a cushion in between my legs while on my knees another—as a way to support the body's balanced and easy opening.

When you are ready to begin, situate yourself in a self-supporting position with your spine upright yet not rigid. It helps to have your hips above the knees and to imagine a cord lifting your head toward the sky.

You can either close your eyes or lower your gaze so you are less distracted by external objects. Invite a relaxed, alert dignity to your posture, and set an intention of sitting for the duration.

Practice: Mindfulness of Breath

Sitting quietly with our eyes closed for even as little as ten or fifteen minutes a day begins to "clear the waste" out of our hearts and minds, making room for the nourishment of peace and wisdom to enter in.

—Brian Browne Walker, The I Ching or Book of Changes

If you're just beginning, sitting for ten minutes is a good starting point. You can gently grow this time up to twenty or thirty minutes or longer as your practice develops.

Set your timer. Give yourself a moment to settle into the space, and gently close your eyes. Take a few deep breaths, and let the breath return to its natural rhythm. Bringing an intentional curious attention to the breath, notice where you feel it most in the body—maybe where the belly expands and contracts, maybe with the rise and fall of the chest and shoulders. You may feel it as it turns the corner of your windpipe or notice it in the nasal passage area. You may sense it at the very opening of the nostrils where it first enters the body and becomes the breath of life, feeling the sensation of the air brushing against the skin on the area of the upper lip. You may feel it expanding and releasing the whole body in concert.

After you discover the place you feel it most, focus your attention and curiosity there while expanding your willingness to be with what you discover.

What do you notice as your attention rests on the breath? Is it fast or slow? Deep or shallow? Long or short? What is its rhythm? Is it stable? Unsteady? Is it labored or flowing easy? Smooth, rough? Thick or thin in texture? Cool or warm?

> *Concentration is an act of cherishing a chosen object.*
>
> *— Sharon Salzberg*

Is the "in" breath equal to the "out" breath? How does it change over time? Where is the point when it is no longer an inhale and becomes an exhale? Is that discernible? What happens as it changes? Does it speed up? Slow down? Get deeper? The exploration is a simple noticing and allowing without any need to change what is happening but rather to observe and experience the changes as they occur.

If you notice your attention has wandered from the breath just gently and nonjudgmentally bring it back to the breath of this moment.

While there are many meditative practices that use intentional breathing in patterns or rhythms, in basic mindfulness practice, we let go of actively directing the breath and, instead, observe it in its natural state. We let the breath just be the breath, as it is, moment to moment.

Each moment during practice offers an opportunity to discover anew the characteristics of the breath. But just as we steady our attention onto the breath, we may soon notice our attention wander. Maybe we start thinking about something we have to do or a conversation we just had with our partner. Wherever our attention goes, this is perfectly natural. It is not uncommon to have our attention to the breath disturbed many times during a session.

In the mindfulness of breath practice, it's of no concern that the mind has wandered or where it wandered to. When we notice it, we just let go and gently guide our awareness back to the present breath. Rather than judging the mind for doing what it does best—think—we can celebrate a moment of wakefulness when we notice our attention is no longer on the breath.

It may help to understand at this point that just as the eye's role is to see and the ear's is to hear, the mind's role is to think, to be aware of other things around us, to plan, to remember, and, of course, to have discernment and opinions about it all. We can tenderly note that thinking is not bad per se but vitally important for living. Without it, we wouldn't be able to function.

What becomes impactful as we undertake our mindfulness practice is exploring firsthand our mind, thinking, and our relationship to our mind and thinking. We may discover that even though the nature of the mind is to think, it does not always think as we want. And it may think when we don't want it to. We may wrestle with this newfound truth that our mind and thoughts are not under our control. This can be quite disconcerting. Try as we might, the mind seems to have a mind of its own.

> *The truth will set you free, but first it will piss you off.*
>
> — *Gloria Steinem*

As we turn a more focused attention to our breath, we'll see that the mind, at times, can be unruly, uncontrollable and inconsolable. We'll explore more of this later, so for now, just noticing that the mind wandered without engaging in the specifics of where it gallivanted to, we can just nod with a gentle knowing and forgiving attitude as we bring our attention back to the breath. At this stage, we purposefully treat all our thoughts as equal and just practice letting go of each of them as we notice them, regardless of their momentary importance or emotional charge.

As we begin our mindfulness practice, we are encouraged to commit to a specific period and sticking to it regardless of how we feel about our experience during the session. If we wait for the perfect circumstances for practice—a calm mind, perfectly quiet surroundings, etc.—we will never gain the invaluable skill of witnessing and sitting through sleepy, restless, doubtful, angry, or desirous times. We'll miss the wisdom that only becomes available from persisting through these difficult circumstances.

So rather than creating a practice of convenience, a firm time commitment made at the beginning of a session not only supports building our mindfulness muscle and the wisdom that develops from the practice but also becomes an exercise in strengthening our ability to disentangle from our thoughts and actions—one of the greatest benefits of a mindfulness practice.

With the support of adopting a nonjudgmental attitude and an intention of meeting what we find with kind acceptance, the process can turn from one of gritting one's teeth to make it through a practice period to an exercise in developing more self-compassion.

And while stillness in the body supports stillness in the mind, it can be difficult and challenging to sit still, whether we're surfing the waves of a busy or angry mind or encountering moments of pain in the body. As part of growing our self-compassion, we can meet these challenges with a tender kindness while still holding to our commitment to sit.

Over time, as your practice and commitment deepen, you can expand the frequency and duration of practice periods. Begin with five to ten minutes three to five days a week and slowly grow the frequency to daily for twenty to thirty minutes.

Focusing and calming the mind, while extremely helpful in themselves, are just the budding edge of the most rewarding features of a mindfulness practice. These qualities also help create the conditions necessary for some of the most beneficial outcomes of mindfulness.

Mindfulness practice develops other helpful factors for living a meaningful life, including wisdom, love, flexibility, and resiliency. For our health, bringing attention to this moment offers the body and mind the space and rest to rebalance itself. Through becoming more restfully aware of what is happening in the moment, our self-regulating systems have the time to do their work, bringing a more alert and peaceful state of being to our body, heart, and mind.

Also, through exploring and investigating what is usually hidden from our normal waking consciousness, we develop a potential to break patterns that no longer serve us. From here, we can consciously work to fashion a more radiant life through actively considering what we want and what brings meaning.

The Eternal Forgiving Nature of This Moment

*This moment doesn't care
that you forgot your breath
a moment ago.*

*That moment is gone
And it didn't care anyway.*

*This moment is busy unfolding.
Are you here?*

*The wind wends through the trees
The sun continues its rise
The birds sing and swing
In morning delight*

*Plants and trees
continue their growth
Your heart beats
Your body breathes*

*This moment doesn't care
that you forgot your breath
a moment ago.*

Why should you?

This moment is busy unfolding.

Are you here?

Emerging Knowledge

Chapter 6

Research Reveals Hope

Researchers' interest in mindfulness practice has steadily increased as studies continue to reveal its beneficial effects.

— Greg Flaxman and Lisa Flook, PhD

I get enraptured studying the effects of mindfulness and compassion in the body and mind through the emerging field of *contemplative neurosciences*. (This field of study focuses on the changes within the brain, mind and body as a result of contemplative practices, such as mindfulness meditation, qigong and yoga.) I understand, though, why some of my clients and students may not share this same enthusiasm. Tending to the details and following the revealed data can be dry and sometimes arduous to absorb.

Suffice it to say that the number of studies on mindfulness is growing by leaps and bounds. In 2005, a mere one hundred research papers had been published on mindfulness. By 2013, some one thousand five hundred were recorded, and by the time you read this, hundreds more will most likely be published.

Most studies cover the many benefits of mindfulness, particularly with stress, stress-related illnesses, well-being, and more. If that's enough for you, feel free to skip onto the next section, but if you're curious about the particulars, read on.

Research is flourishing because there are several hundred mindfulness-based programs in hospitals, medical centers, clinics, and universities in the United States alone. Mindfulness-related activity was found at 79 percent of medical schools in the United States in 2014.[4] Embedding mindfulness in institutions prepared for scientific research is an advantage to discovering and recording its benefits firsthand.

Mindfulness has also become one of the most efficacious methods used in psychology today for a variety of conditions. For the emerging field of *positive psychology,* which focuses on enriching the good rather than focusing on what is wrong, mindfulness is at the core.

Mindfulness Takes Center Stage

Studies in the early 1970s, such as that by Dr. Herbert Benson of the Harvard Medical School, demonstrated that *transcendental meditation,* a meditation practice that uses the repetition of a sound, produced a pattern of significant physiological changes that he termed the *relaxation response.* This study also supported the benefits of mindfulness. Since these early studies, so much more has been learned about the benefits of mindfulness, mindfulness-based practices, and compassion practices.

Jon Kabat-Zinn, PhD, founder of *mindfulness-based stress reduction (MBSR)* at the University of Massachusetts, broke ground for scientific research on the benefits of mindfulness in the late 1970s. His evidence-based research showed "consistent, reliable, and reproducible demonstrations of major and clinically relevant reductions in medical

---

[4]   Barnes, N., Hattan, P., Black, D. S., et al. (2016) Mindfulness. doi:10.1007/s12671-016-0623-8

and psychological symptoms across a wide range of medical diagnoses." Dr. Kabat-Zinn's work showed improvements for those experiencing chronic pain and other medical diagnoses and for medical patients with a secondary diagnosis of anxiety and/or panic.[5]

Clinical research indicates that mindfulness is associated with reduced emotional distress, more positive states of mind, and a better quality of life. In addition, mindfulness practice influences not only the brain but also the autonomic nervous system, stress hormones, and immune system in helpful ways. Moreover, health-related behaviors, including eating, sleeping, and substance abuse are benefited by the practice.

Let's take a glimpse at how mindfulness affects our neural structures and other physio-based aspects of our being to better understand why it is so promising for so many people.

Mindfulness and the Brain

Mindfulness helps shift activity in the brain from the default narrative network to the direct experience network. Both networks are important, but we gain more richness, aliveness and accurate perceptions when we tap into the direct experience of this moment.

— Based on the work of David Rock

Current research indicates that mindfulness affects the structural and neural patterns in the brain. In a study conducted in 2005, results showed thicker cortical regions related to attention and sensory processing in long-term *insight meditation* participants. (*Insight*

---

[5]   http://www.umassmed.edu/cfm/mindfulness-based-programs/mbsr-courses/about-mbsr/history-of-mbsr/

meditation or *Vipassana* are terms sometimes used for mindfulness practices.) The study noted differences were most pronounced in older participants, suggesting that this meditation practice may impact age-related declines in cortical thickness.[6]

This research most poignantly points to the brain's ability to be changed by experience and, in this case, our focused experience. This is known as *neural-plasticity,* which refers to changes in neural pathways and synapses resulting from changes in behavior, environment, neural processes, thinking, emotions, and even bodily injury.

Tests performed on the brains of meditators completing an eight-week course on mindfulness revealed an apparent shrinking of the *amygdala,* the region of the brain associated with fear and, evolutionarily, where our stress response of fight, flight, or freeze originates. Interestingly, the connection between the amygdala and the *prefrontal cortex* region (our most evolved brain region that promotes our highest cognitive functioning and regulates our thoughts, actions, and emotions) strengthens the longer that one has been practicing mindfulness.[7] This means that our instinctual reaction to stressful situations can possibly be replaced by more thoughtful responses.

According to a 2009 article in *Nature Reviews,* stress "can cause a rapid and dramatic loss of prefrontal cognitive abilities."[8] A fascinating feedback loop affecting our response to stress may be created from practicing mindfulness. Since mindfulness strengthens our ability to respond from our prefrontal cortex and decreases the amygdala's control

---

[6]   Lazar, S. W., Kerr, C. E., Wasserman, R. H., Gray, J. R., Greve, D. N., Treadway, M. T., … Fischl, B. (2005). Meditation experience is associated with increased cortical thickness. *Neuroreport, 16*(17), 1893–1897. Retrieved from http://www.ncbi.nlm.nih.gov/pmc/articles/PMC1361002/

[7]   What does mindfulness meditation do to your brain? Blogs. (2014, June 12). Retrieved May 14, 2015, from http://blogs.scientificamerican.com/guest-blog/what-does-mindfulness-meditation-do-to-your-brain/

[8]   Arnsten, A. F. T. (2009). Stress signaling pathways that impair prefrontal cortex structure and function. Nature Reviews. *Neuroscience, 10*(6), 410–422. http://doi.org/10.1038/nrn2648

over our response, this new way of responding to stress over time may lessen the loss of prefrontal cognitive abilities under stressful situations. This, in turn, strengthens our ability to respond to stress less reactively, which then lessens the loss of our prefrontal cognitive abilities and so on. It will be fascinating to learn over time how this affects our physiological evolution with stress.

There is new research around how we think about stress and the influence those thoughts have on our body. Through an engaging TED talk, Stanford University psychologist Kelly McGonigal helps us understand the role attitude plays with stress and our physical health. Basically, whether we perceive stress to be negative or positive has an effect on our physical health according to recent studies. Seeing that mindfulness can increase our ability to rework our thoughts and opinions, it has the potential to play an immensely valuable role in contributing to our health.

When it comes to cognitive function and comprehension, one study indicated that with just two weeks of training in mindfulness, participants experienced increased reading comprehension scores, decreased mind wandering, and increased working memory capacity.[9]

The direct effect mindfulness has on the brain, both physically and in functionality, is increasingly evident. This is an important thing to recognize as we may have more power over our health and wellness than we ever thought possible. The fact that we can actually change our physiology by how we think and that change in physiology alters how we think and experience our lives and so on is profound. It's knowledge we can begin to use immediately to better our lives.

---

[9] Mrazek, M. D., Franklin, M. S., Phillips, D. T., Baird, B., & Schooler, J. W. (2013). Mindfulness training improves working memory capacity and GRE performance while reducing mind wandering. *Psychological Science, 24*(5), 776–781. http://doi.org/10.1177/0956797612459659

Chapter 7

What about the Difficulties?

Mindfulness not only reduces stress but also gently builds an inner strength so that future stressors have less impact on our happiness and physical well-being.

— *Shamash Alidina*

Our bodies are hardwired to respond to immediate threats with protective strategies evolved over millennia. Our ancestors who dodged immediate threats from predators and aggressors passed along important genes for our survival. They are still expressed today anytime we perceive a threat to either our physical bodies or our sense of self.

This autonomic reaction is most commonly known as the *stress response* and is filled with biochemical reactions lasting anywhere from microseconds to minutes. When tension builds from a stressful situation, we have an enormous storehouse of strength, wits, and energy at our disposal to fend off immediate danger. Once the danger passes, our bodies shift back to a calm, balanced state of health and awareness.

In today's world of stress, though, we *rarely* have the need for such a strong physical reaction. For the average person, there are fewer saber-toothed tigers, large raptors, and bears in our midst.

So why is stress growing? Why do our present-day stressors seem to come more often and last for longer periods? It could be because we are more identified with a sense of self than our ancestors were and perceived threats to this identity lead us to the same physical reaction as an actual threat to our body. Also, today we have more identities to protect, such as our job-related identity, family or romantic identity, or who we are in community.

In any case, because of our fast-paced lifestyle, this results in fewer periods of recovery when our bodies can rest and regain a relaxed, alert balance. As a result, our bodies remain bathed in biochemicals that can actually cause harm to us in the long run.

Today the "fight, flight, or freeze" reaction to threat that originates in the amygdala, or our *reptilian brain*, can contribute to stress-related illnesses. Here's why:

When we encounter a perceived threat, such as being surprised by a large dog running toward us or a car veering in front of us, our hypothalamus, a tiny region at the base of our brain, sets off an alarm system in our body that activates nerve and hormonal signals. Our adrenal glands release a surge of hormones, including *adrenaline* and *cortisol*.

Adrenaline increases our heart rate, elevates our blood pressure, and boosts energy supplies, which help us either fend off or run from the danger. Cortisol, the primary stress hormone, increases sugars (glucose) in the bloodstream, enhances our brain's use of glucose, and increases the availability of substances that repair tissues.

At the same time, cortisol curbs nonessential functions in a perceived life-threatening situation. It alters immune system responses and suppresses the digestive and reproductive systems and growth processes. This makes perfect sense as these systems are not critical for survival during a true life-threatening emergency. In microseconds, our energy is concentrated to survive the present threat.

Once the immediate threat is over, the hormones return to normal levels, which leads to systems returning to normal baseline rates and activities. The problem comes when we are under excessive pressure, which hurried, active, and stressful lifestyles can lead to. In these situations, the body doesn't get to return to healthy *stasis* — a period of equilibrium.

Today a lot of *stressors* (conditions or stimulus that creates stress) are persistent, leading to difficulties during the stress event itself and, accumulatively, in the body's overused systems. If there is never a break for these systems to fully recover, over time, their ability to function healthily will diminish.

So coupling our inborn biological response with present-day stress events can lead to a long-term activation of the stress-response system, or *chronic stress,* which can include overexposure to cortisol and other stress hormones. Prolonged exposure to stress can lead to some of the following ailments:

- High blood pressure
- Heart disease
- Digestive problems
- Sleep problems
- Anxiety
- Depression
- Weight change
- Memory and concentration impairment
- Inflammation
- Immune disorders

Each of these conditions are prevalent in our fast-paced cultures.

Anxiety disorders, such as PTSD, obsessive-compulsive disorder, panic disorder, and generalized anxiety disorder (GAD) affect about 18 percent of the American adult population and about 8 percent of teens aged thirteen to eighteen.[10] In 2002, anxiety disorder was declared the most common mental illness in the United States, affecting some nineteen million Americans.[11] This is a growing concern in modern-day life as the conditions for our recovery from stressful situations are getting further out of reach. Additionally, the lower on the economic ladder we are, the harder we work to meet our basic needs, and the less time we have for leisure and rest—those things we need for recovery.

In contrast, a simple breathing technique called the *relaxation response* creates a different biochemical response to stress. This method developed by Dr. Herbert Benson—professor, author, cardiologist, and founder of Harvard's mind/body medical institute—is now taught in major hospitals and clinical programs. It signals to the body that it is safe to relax and engages the parasympathetic nervous system, slowing down organs and muscles and increasing blood flow to the brain.[12]

Mindfulness practice helps combat stress, anxiety, and depressive disorders because the attention is focused on the activity of interest in the present moment, where, in general, immediate threats are few and where the mind has little room to run off with potential catastrophic scenarios.

In addition to our natural stress response, the body's ability to *self-regulate* its systems is also adversely affected while under stress. Self-regulation is important for maintaining not only the stability of system functioning but also our ability to adapt to new circumstances.

---

[10] Stress on disease. Carnegie Mellon University. (n.d.). Retrieved April 28, 2015, from http://www.cmu.edu/homepage/health/2012/spring/stress-on-disease.shtml

[11] Are you too anxious? *Time*. (n.d.). Retrieved April 28, 2015, from http://content.time.com/time/magazine/article/0,9171,1002606,00.html

[12] Dr. Herbert Benson's relaxation response. (n.d.). Retrieved December 30, 2017, from http://www.psychologytoday.com/blog/heart-and-soul-healing/201303/dr-herbert-benson-s-relaxation-response

The more stressed we are, the less our ability to adapt to a changing environment, potentially leading to a need to control our surroundings, including people and routines.

This became evident in the workplaces of those affected by the catastrophic fires of 2014–2017 in Lake County, California, where I consulted on disaster resiliency. For one organization, the majority were directly affected by the fires, having either lost their home or had family or close friends lose theirs. In addition, because the organization was dealing directly with the cleanup and subsequent rebuild, dramatic changes in work load and work systems added more stress to this already traumatized population. As well, some of the staff were dealing directly with other traumatized people trying to rebuild their lives.

As a tool of resilience following a disaster, regaining a sense of control over our environment and life is important. Any change has a tendency to create even more stress and uncomfortable feelings of being out of control. Sustained episodes of stress can actually create more stress as we lose our flexibility, and triggers can extend periods of the body's stress response, opening the path to potential illnesses. This ever-tightening loop of trigger and response can lead to generally anxious moods and potential emotional and physical breakdowns during otherwise nonstressful times.

As part of the trainings, I introduced mindfulness practices as one of many tools that can help mitigate the body's reaction to stress because mindfulness supports our ability to be more present and flexible. By training our attention to be more accepting and focused in the current moment, mounting stresses can be avoided.

Mindfulness supports our ability to be more present and flexible.

In a *meta-analysis* (an analysis of combined data from multiple studies) on the effects of MBSR, study results suggest the usefulness of mindfulness for a broad range of chronic disorders. This indicates it may have an effect on coping skills in general as well as under extraordinary conditions of serious disorder or stress, which can come about during disasters.[13]

What's more, evidence shows a reduction in respiratory rate for mindfulness practitioners.[14] This points to a relaxed body and possibly a heart that has to work less to circulate more oxygen. The ongoing practice of mindfulness increases our resilience from stress and changes our physiological response to stress. If we are able to choose a life of peace and serenity, the stressors that eventually lead to illness can be minimized. But if we live a life in the modern-day hustle and bustle as most of us do, a practice of mindfulness is a wise response by helping us garner inner and outer resources in a system of support to diminish potential long-term negative impacts of living under constant stress.

Stress, Intention and Immunity

According to a large body of evidence, meditation appears to have profound effects on immune function in health and disease because of its ability to reduce stress.

— David R. Vago, PhD

Have you ever noticed when you are the busiest or most stressed, you seem to get sick? Well, as we explored earlier, stress is *immunosuppressive*— meaning it suppresses the body's immune response. According to Dr. David Vago, an associate psychologist in the functional neuroimaging

---

[13] Grossman, P., Niemann, L., Schmidt, S., & Walach, H. (2004). Mindfulness-based stress reduction and health benefits: A meta-analysis. *Journal of Psychosomatic Research, 57,* 35–43.

[14] Lazar, S. W., Kerr, C. E., Wasserman, R. H., Gray, J. R., Greve, D. N., Treadway, M. T., ... Fischl, B. (2005). Meditation experience is associated with increased cortical thickness. *Neuroreport, 16*(17), 1893–1897. Retrieved from http://www.ncbi.nlm.nih.gov/pmc/articles/PMC1361002/

laboratory at Brigham and Women's Hospital and instructor at Harvard Medical School, mindfulness provides both protection and recovery from stress, which can prevent stress from negatively affecting our immune system.

In a 2008 study of women in early stages of breast cancer, those that participated in an eight-week mindfulness-based stress reduction (MBSR) course showed reduced cortisol levels, improved quality of life, and increased coping effectiveness as compared to those in the study that didn't participate in MBSR. Equally important, the women who participated showed beneficial effects on their immune function as evidenced in reestablished levels of natural killer (NK) cell activity and *cytokine* production levels.[15] Cytokine are cell-signaling molecules that aid cell-to-cell communication in immune responses and stimulate the movement of cells toward sites of inflammation, infection, and trauma. These are two important factors for dealing with cancer.

In another study with HIV patients in 2013, mindfulness-based cognitive therapy (MBCT) participants reported improved quality of life and lessened psychological stress, depressive symptoms, and anxiety symptoms. But most importantly, they showed a significant increase in CD4 cells.[16] (These are *T cells*, a type of white blood cell that fights off disease, viruses, and bacteria.)

So not only does stress contribute to creating disease, but it also makes us more susceptible to viral and bacterial attacks through the suppression of our immune system. Reducing stress opens back up the body's natural healing systems to fend off attacks and help restore health.

---

[15] Witek-Janusek, L., Albuquerque, K., Chroniak, K. R., Chroniak, C., Durazo-Arvizu, R., & Mathews, H. L. (2008). Effect of mindfulness based stress reduction on immune function, quality of life and coping in women newly diagnosed with early stage breast cancer. *Brain, Behavior, and Immunity, 22*(6), 969–981. http://doi.org/10.1016/j.bbi.2008.01.012

[16] Marian Gonzalez-Garcia, M. J. F. (2013). Effectiveness of mindfulness-based cognitive therapy on the quality of life, emotional status, and CD4 cell count of patients aging with HIV infection. *AIDS and Behavior, 18*(4). http://doi.org/10.1007/s10461-013-0612-z

It makes sense to think that any practice that relieves stress will help the autoimmune system function better.

Mindfulness when coupled with conscious intention seems to add an extra edge to relaxation techniques. In my early years of practicing *Reiki*—a supportive healing modality that facilitates deep relaxation—I tried to discover how it worked. It baffled me that the simple act of laying hands on a body (or not, as is the case in distance Reiki) with an intention to heal could actually work, but time and again, I witnessed, experienced, and heard of beneficial results.

My inquiry to understand how Reiki worked exposed me to a wide span of some very different approaches to reality. As I explored the metaphysical to quantum physics, one thing became clear: while there may not be evidence that supports anything "supernatural" with Reiki, the very act of getting to a point of deep relaxation allows the body's innate and extraordinary intelligence to get to work on healing itself.

Our body is one of nature's most successful self-regulating systems that may need nothing more than to give it enough time in a relaxed state to heal itself from a variety of ailments. Mindfulness is proven to reduce stress. Evidence supports Reiki's ability to help relieve stress.[17] Studies continue to reveal the truth behind the seemingly miraculous healing capabilities of the body. And as explored earlier, how we think about what is happening does, in fact, affect how it impacts us.

In the case of Reiki and in remembering McGonigal's work on how our opinions on stress affect the body, I surmise intention and beliefs of both the Reiki practitioner and the recipient toward health and wellness play a contributing role. Adding conscious intention to any relaxation practice may help create a perfect recipe to support *all* the body's systems in optimal functioning.

Guided imagery, a practice where one is led to create sensory-rich mental images, is just one technique used in setting intention and

---

[17]   Wardell, D. W., & Engebretson, J. (2001). Biological correlates of Reiki Touch's healing. *Journal of Advanced Nursing, 33*, 439–445. doi:10.1046/j.1365-2648.2001.01691.x

has been shown to be successful in increasing the immune response in cancer patients.[18] Consciously setting intention toward health and reinforcing that with the immunoprotective and recovery benefits of mindfulness show great promise in reducing the effects of stress on our body's susceptibility to illness and disease. Together they foster a healthy immune system.

Depression and Anxiety

Depression is not only the most common mental illness, it's also one of the most tenacious. Up to 80 percent of people who experience a major depressive episode may relapse. Drugs may lose their effectiveness over time, if they work at all.

— Stacy Lu, American Psychological Association, Monitor on Psychology

There is a growing body of evidence supporting the efficacy of mindfulness-based therapies for relieving *depression* and *anxiety* disorders. Depression is a mental condition characterized by feelings of despondency and dejection. Anxiety is characterized by feelings of worry and unease, particularly about something unknown or in the future.

The results of studies are so promising that a whole new psychological approach, *mindfulness-based cognitive therapy (MBCT)*, has emerged. It combines *cognitive therapy* (a therapeutic approach that includes challenging negative thinking patterns about the self and the world) with mindfulness practices, attitudes, and approaches to shift the

---

[18] [18] Naparstek, B. (2011, December 30). The science behind guided imagery. Retrieved April 20, 2016, from http://www.huffingtonpost.com/belleruth-naparstek/guided-imagery-cancer-patients_b_1026296.html

patient's relationship with their thoughts. It is designed to help those suffering repeated bouts of depression and chronic unhappiness.[19]

Because depression and anxiety are mood disorders that show up in the thinking mind, it isn't difficult to see how mindfulness can play a helpful role. As we shift our relationship with the mind and thoughts as we'll discover later, the grip certain emotionally charged thoughts hold on us loosens. By cultivating a more spacious attitude and allowance with our thoughts, how they impact our experience changes. The roominess affords more ease, choice, and freedom of response.

In a 2002 *Time Magazine* article by Christine Gorman, *anxiety disorder* was noted as being one of the most common mental illnesses in the United States.[20] According to health experts, it becomes a *disorder* when it persists to the point of interfering in one's life.

It turns out that women are 60 percent more likely than men and non-Hispanic whites are more likely than Hispanic or non-Hispanic Blacks to experience anxiety disorder in their lifetime according to the National Institute of Mental Health.[21]

It's important to remember that anxiety, our response to perceived threats, is hardwired into our biology and is one of the mechanisms that have helped our species survive to the present day. Anxious thoughts, such as "Do we have enough food to get through the winter?" "Is this the path the saber-toothed tiger takes to the drinking hole?" and so on, were much needed at one point in our evolutionary history. However, Gorman notes, "While it is a normal response to physical danger—and can be a useful tool for focusing the mind when there's a deadline looming—anxiety becomes a problem when it persists too long beyond the immediate threat."

---

[19] Your guide to mindfulness-based cognitive therapy. (n.d.). Retrieved April 26, 2017, from http://mbct.com/

[20] Gorman, C. (2002, June 10). The science of anxiety. *Time*. Retrieved from http://content.time.com/time/magazine/article/0,9171,1002605,00.html

[21] https://www.nimh.nih.gov/health/statistics/prevalence/any-anxiety-disorder-among-adults.shtml

Mindfulness can be seen as an antidote to anxiety because our focus is anchored in the present moment experience where things are most likely safe and benign. We can't experience anxiety and relaxation at the same time.

While anxiety is one of today's most common mental illnesses, *depression* is the most prevalent and debilitating. It is ranked by the World Health Organization as the leading cause of disability globally.[22] It affects up to fourteen million adults each year with an estimated thirty-two to thirty-five million United States residents expected to develop the disorder at some point in their lifetime.[23]

Up to 80 percent of the individuals who experience a major depressive episode may relapse. This points to potential ongoing and painful emotional cycles for many people. Pharmaceuticals can be helpful, but they can lose their effectiveness over time if they work at all for particular individuals, and patients may be concerned about long-term side effects.

Cognitive therapy has been shown to be as effective as medication in treating depression and has reduced the incidence of relapse.[24] Moreover, MBCT was found to be as effective a treatment for depression relapse as was relapse-maintenance medication in a study by Oxford University professor Willem Kuyken, PhD, and colleagues.[25] This study also indicated that MBCT had a larger effect on those suffering from more

---

[22] Mindfulness therapy as good as medication for chronic depression - study. (2015, April 20). Reuters. Retrieved from http://www.reuters.com/article/2015/04/20/us-health-depression-idUSKBN0NB2KO20150420

[23] Nat Rev Neurosci. 2008 October 9(10): 788–796. Published online 2008 September 11. doi: 10.1038/nrn2345

[24] Nat Rev Neurosci. 2008 October 9(10): 788–796. Published online 2008 September 11. doi: 10.1038/nrn2345

[25] Kuyken, W. (2008). Mindfulness-based cognitive therapy to prevent relapse in recurrent depression. *Journal of Consulting and Clinical Psychology, 76*(6), 966–978. http://doi.org/10.1037/a0013786

severe childhood abuses—a greater risk indicator for relapses. This is promising news for those afflicted with depression.

Besides my personal experience with situational depression, working with and witnessing friends, family members, clients and loved ones has fostered a deep compassion for those who struggle with depression's torment and agony.

That compassion and my own experience with depression partly drive my passion to teach mindfulness. Shortly after my dog Shyla passed, a depressive melancholy settled in. It eventually turned into a daily struggle to fight the lethargy that settled deep into my bones. I had no real reason to get out of bed in the morning. Not only was no one depending on me for care, but there was also no one sharing my experience anymore.

Even though I was in a loving, supportive, and committed relationship, I was never more deeply alone on the inside.

Months after her death, while traveling around Yosemite on my first summer excursion without her, thoughts of ending my life surfaced. Virtually every summer for the previous fifteen years was spent gallivanting with her exploring some new destination. Taking this trip alone felt really empty and void of purpose. There was no motivation to explore.

Driving slowly behind a line of cars into the park one morning, I started thinking about how easily I could turn my car over into the Merced River and end my life. The embankment was steep enough, and the river close and deep enough that by veering off just the right way down the embankment, the car would roll, flip, and land top down in the river. Since I was wearing a seatbelt, I reasoned, it would keep me immersed under water long enough to drown before someone could come to the rescue.

Thank goodness for my mindfulness practice and recovery work. When these thoughts became conscious, I knew I was in trouble.

The mindfulness helped me to see the thoughts as they arose. With enough space between thought and response, I didn't allow the precise, persistent images and heavy emotions to culminate in a quick jerk of the steering wheel. It saved me from creating the simple and quick death scene manifesting in my mind's eye.

My recovery work helped me know it was time to reach out. When I arrived back at the hostel, I quickly called a few close friends for support. I also wrote in my journal, which helped bring the thoughts and emotions to the surface. I compassionately held space as the tears and mournful thoughts arose and passed. Knowing it was a difficult time, I instinctively created a container of loving compassion to witness and hold space with this tender and tense emotional episode.

I continued on with the trip, taking long hikes and giving myself all the time and space I needed to grieve. It brought to light my changing relationship with Shyla. She was physically gone but would never be gone from my heart and life. The journey became richer with emotional warmth for both her and me, all because I didn't impulsively act or run from what was happening.

Simple nurturing strategies such as these can have profound effects during times of distress. Dr. Emma Seppala,[26] associate director at Stanford University's Center for Compassion and Altruism Research and Education, has worked with the Project Welcome Home Troops,[27] teaching yoga- and meditation-based interventions to help returning veterans reduce symptoms of anxiety, anger, insomnia, and depression. She advocates that while we are unable to talk ourselves out of difficult states, something as simple as taking a deep breath begins a physiological response in the body that shifts the state. As we learned earlier, breath can be used to help shift and regulate emotional states, and it's at the core of mindfulness practices.

With the potential MBCT shows, those struggling with recurrent depression and debilitating anxiety have a simple but powerful tool to

---

[26]   http://www.emmaseppala.com/

[27]   http://www.projectwelcomehometroops.org/

help find their way to more comfort and ease. And once we stop the pain, we can then focus our attention to growing the joy and fulfillment in life, leading to a greater chance for happiness.

Addiction

Mindfulness practice helps us develop the capacity to see clearly exactly what we're attached to so that we can let go of it and end our suffering.

— *Ronald Alexander, PhD*

Mindfulness shows promise for those of us afflicted with addictive and compulsive behaviors, especially because of the strong relationship between stress, addiction, and persistent compulsive thoughts that accompany addictive patterns. The active practice of mindfully and nonjudgmentally observing thoughts as we'll learn increases our attention and allows *equanimity* to grow in all areas of our life. Equanimity, that calm, level-headed composure, gives rise to a more varied set of responses to competing desires. We're more capable of fending off the clamoring of immediate emotional or physical wants and direct our energies and attention toward healthier choices that align with our long-term health intentions and well-being. We're better able to monitor, evaluate, and modify our behavior as a result.

When it comes to addiction-relapse prevention, targeted mindfulness practices may strengthen the ability for recovering addicts to monitor and skillfully cope with the hardship associated with cravings and negative emotions.[28] This makes practical sense; as we practice mindfulness, we learn to sit with what arises, absent of critical evaluation. With our

---

[28] Bowen, S., Witkiewitz, K., Clifasefi, S. L., & et al. (2014). Relative efficacy of mindfulness-based relapse prevention, standard relapse prevention, and treatment as usual for substance use disorders: A randomized clinical trial. *JAMA Psychiatry, 71*(5), 547–556. http://doi.org/10.1001/jamapsychiatry.2013.4546

gentle, focused attention, we notice a thought, sensation, or emotion arises and eventually passes away. From this repeated practice, we learn directly that we do not need to suppress or modify these experiences as they are temporary and short-lived.

For an addict, the craving in the body can show up like an *urgent need*. According to Dr. Jill Bolte Taylor, a Harvard-trained and published neuroanatomist, emotions last about ninety seconds from the inception of the chemical reaction in the body until the chemicals are fully flushed out—that is, if we don't feed or replay the story around the emotion. Otherwise, it can continue to manifest and remanifest.

Like emotions, cravings unfold over time and are shown to be responsive to similar techniques used to regulate emotions.[29] This suggests positive indications for mindfulness as a tool to help moderate and ease the difficulties of cravings. While it may not replace the need for medically supervised detoxification, as our mindfulness practice strengthens, those "urgent needs" become just another series of intense waves of experience in a sea of happenings.

> *Emotions last about ninety seconds from the inception of the chemical reaction in the body until the chemicals are fully flushed out—that is, if we don't feed or replay the story around the emotion.*

Comfortable or uncomfortable, as we practice mindfulness, our refined attention begins to pick up on subtle variations. Unpacking the concept of "pain" or "craving" or "withdrawal" reveals a richly woven fabric of sensations. We acknowledge the sensation, accept the truth of its existence, and choose our response wisely. With practice, we learn to ride the temporary waves of any sensation—pleasant, unpleasant, or neutral.

---

[29] Giuliani, N. R., & Berkman, E. T. (2015). Craving is an affective state and its regulation can be understood in terms of the extended process model of emotion regulation. *Psychological Inquiry, 26*(1), 48–53. https://doi.org/10.1080/10478 40X.2015.955072

This deepening awareness facilitated by a mindfulness practice was critical when I stopped smoking tobacco in my late thirties. I had smoked since I was a young teen, wanting to be "cool" and showing my "adultness."

My smoking habit quickly turned into a coping mechanism for managing the unmanageable.

Because of the stigma attached, smoking also helped me grow a perpetual pattern of isolation, low self-esteem, and crippling shame.

I tried hundreds if not thousands of times to quit, but it wasn't until I had enough mindfulness practice and recovery under my belt that I was able to successfully and lovingly sit through the various withdrawal symptoms over the course of the first four days of quitting. I was new in recovery at the time and was haphazardly though eagerly learning how to experience emotions while sober for the first time in my adult life.

Mindfulness helped me let go of one of the most addictive substances known, and results in one study support the use of it for tobacco withdrawal. This study showed mindfulness had a 4 percent more effectiveness rate than the American Lung Association's Freedom from Smoking program. Additionally, there was evidence of sustained success at a seventeen-week follow up session.[30] It is believed that these favorable results may be because of the fact that mindfulness decouples our experience from our actions, giving us more freedom of choice in our response.

Cravings do not necessarily have to lead to acting out in an addiction. The disconnect of experience from automatic reaction is a key component of how mindfulness can bring benefit across a variety of areas in our lives and, particularly, its potential effectiveness for overcoming addictions and compulsions.

---

[30] Brewer, J. A., Mallik, S., Babuscio, T. A., Nich, C., Johnson, H. E., Deleone, C. M., . . . Rounsaville, B. J. (2011). Mindfulness training for smoking cessation: Results from a randomized controlled trial. *Drug and Alcohol Dependence, 119*(1–2), 72–80. http://doi.org/10.1016/j.drugalcdep.2011.05.027

Chapter 8

Growing Wellness and Joy

Mindfulness and Well-being

The conscious ability to transform an individual's mind is perhaps the greatest ability humans have at hand to shape the direction of their lives and positively affect the lives of others around them.

— Kelly Zarcone

When I was very young, I, like many children, held each day with joy and hope. The curious and innocent aliveness coursed through my tiny being, giving rise to days of wonder and delight. But by the time I was seventeen, an optimism-crushing cynicism developed, and I fell prey to what's known as the *negativity bias* that was fed almost daily with a hypercritical and sometimes raging father.

The negativity bias is that ever-vigilant and necessary part of our evolved biology that effortlessly remembers negative and harmful experiences much more easily than positive ones. It's designed to keep us safe from harm, which has helped our species survive over the millennium. As part of that, we are hardwired to notice what is wrong and what can potentially go wrong, and we do this assessment in a virtually unconscious split second.

I learned to spend my days, much like my father, critiquing everyone and everything, putting harsh emphasis on how *idiotic* someone was for their *asinine* actions. This attitude and outlook toward others and life, while an important part of our survival, grew to eventually take its toll on my very *well-being*.

Well-being is basically where we are in our level of comfort, health, and happiness. Many spiritual, psychological, and wisdom traditions place emphasis on the importance of the *quality* of consciousness to maintain and enhance our well-being according to Ken Wilber of the Integral Institute,[31] and research supports this.

> *Our well-being is made up of a set of skills that can be learned and developed.*

Dr. Richard Davidson, founder of the Center for Healthy Minds at the University of Wisconsin, Madison, gives credence to the idea that our well-being is made up of a set of *skills* that can be learned and developed.[32]

The key attributes in our well-being, according to Davidson, are

- *resilience*, or how rapidly we are able to recover from adversity;
- *outlook* (attitude), or the ability to recognize and cherish the positive in others and experiences;

---

[31] Wilber, K. (2000). Integral psychology: Consciousness, spirit, psychology, therapy. Shambhala Publications.

[32] Davidson, R. J. (n.d.). The four constituents of well-being. Retrieved May 6, 2016, from http://greatergood.berkeley.edu/gg_live/mindfulness_well_being_at_work/speaker/richard_davidson/four_constituents_of_well-being

- *attention*, or awareness of what we are doing as we are doing it (mindfulness); and
- *generosity*, or altruistic behavior.

These fundamental components of well-being can be shaped, molded, and strengthened through training and experience. Mindfulness and compassion practices actively engage three of them—outlook (attitude), attention (mindfulness), and generosity—which results in the fourth, resilience.

In reviewing research on mindfulness, Dr. Jeffrey M. Greeson found many study outcomes associating mindfulness with less emotional distress, more positive states of mind, and a better quality of life.[33]

We've explored how a mindfulness practice can positively influence the brain, the autonomic nervous system, stress, the immune system, and health behaviors, including eating, sleeping, and using substances. We've also seen that cultivating greater attention, awareness, and acceptance through meditation practice is also associated with lower levels of psychological distress, including areas of anxiety, depression, anger, and worry. Research also suggests that people with higher levels of mindfulness are better able to contribute to their sense of well-being through greater emotional awareness, understanding, acceptance, and the ability to shift or "repair" unpleasant mood states.

Greeson's review also discloses that people with higher natural levels of mindfulness—whether through formal training and practice or not—report feeling "more joyful, inspired, grateful, hopeful, content, vital, and satisfied with life."[34]

According to the research, just being in a momentary state of mindfulness is associated with a greater sense of well-being.

---

[33] Greeson, J. M. (2009). Mindfulness research update: 2008. *Complementary Health Practice Review*, *14*(1), 10. http://doi.org/10.1177/1533210108329862

[34] Ibid.

In another study conducted at Northern Arizona University and published in the *Journal of Happiness Studies*[35] (a scientific journal focused on well-being and quality of life), research brought to light that mindfulness practice was not only related to decreases in unfavorable psychological symptoms (including the family of neurosis—depression, stress, anxiety, and obsessiveness) but contributed to increases in health, subjective well-being, and resilience.[36] As well, openness to experience, conscientiousness, agreeableness, and self-compassion were noted in some of the studies.[37]

I was tickled to discover the *Journal of Happiness Studies*. Think of it, we are shifting our focus from what is not working—the psychological array of disorders—to what is positive in our experience and how we can grow that. We are *formally studying* well-being and happiness.

What's really exciting to me is how scientific evidence is pointing to numerous ways that bring about positive states of being *that we can do for ourselves*. So rather than focusing our attention on happiness that is somewhere *out there*—a happiness given to us by someone or something outside ourselves or at some point in the future—we can instead look to this moment and our own capacity to cultivate more positive states of being. What a shift of direction for our attention and energies!

Wisdom traditions throughout the ages have long encouraged a path of attention inward to receive the greatest benefits available in our human experience. Science is now exploring those actions and discovering some pretty amazing insights, including that we have a lot to offer toward influencing and directing our own happiness and well-being.

We each have what is referred to in psychology as a general mood *set point*. This is where we rest in our mood and outlook when not activated

---

[35] Wayment, H., Wiist, B., Sullivan, B., & Warren, M. (2010). Doing and being: Mindfulness, health, and quiet ego characteristics among Buddhist practitioners. *Journal of Happiness Studies, 2011*(12), 575–589. http://doi.org/10.1007/s10902-010-9218-6

[36] Ibid.

[37] Ibid.

by either a positive or negative experience. It's our neutral point and can actually be measured through *magnetic resonance imaging* (MRI), a medical imaging technique that uses strong magnetic fields, electric field gradients, and radio waves to generate images of the organs in the body.

When we're in a positive mood, the left prefrontal cortex is activated, and the amygdala region is quiet, which is reflected in the imaging. When someone is agitated, angry, or stressed, the amygdala and right prefrontal cortex region are activated, and the left side quiet. When not activated by either a positive or negative experience, we can see our unencumbered *set point*.

In a study conducted in 2003, doctors Richard Davidson and Jon Kabat-Zinn discovered that within a few months of beginning a mindfulness practice via an MBSR course, the set point of the participants moved more to the left prefrontal cortex region, or in the "feel-good positive zone."[38]

The implications are astounding that something as simple as paying more attention to our present moment experience with an attitude of acceptance and kindness cannot only generate positive mood feelings in the moment but, in a very short time, can create a more general positive mood and outlook on life over all. It's almost as if we have our happiness and well-being in our own hands. Dare I say it—

We create our own reality.

Okay, I've said it. I don't say these things so that we can judge and see how we're failing ourselves, that we're not happy in life and we're to blame but, instead, to encourage us to begin exploring for ourselves. What happens when we undertake a scientifically proven way to bring about better health and well-being?

---

[38] Davidson, R. J., Kabat-Zinn, J., et al. (2003). Alterations in brain and immune function produced by mindfulness meditation. PubMed – NCBI. *Psychosomatic Medicine, 65*(4), 564–570. Retrieved from http://www.ncbi.nlm.nih.gov/pubmed/12883106

There's an image I remember from my recovery work, and it is that of a person having dug themselves into a deep, dark, and lonely pit, tunneling further down each day into pain and self-harm with seemingly no end in sight. Beginning a mindfulness practice shifts the attention and action from digging deeper to, first, stopping and noticing the harm and, second, choosing a different action. Hopefully one more loving and caring.

We may not end up in some sublime state of bliss,
but at least we've stopped digging.

And stopping the digging is the beginning of stopping the pain. Mindfulness gives us a tool to stop digging and start cultivating health and wellness by taking steps to see the hole and start the climb toward the light. We don't know where we'll end up, but at least we're moving in the better direction.

As for the negatively focused young girl I used to be, I'm not a *Pollyanna* where I am always positive, always feeling bliss or joy, but I can more readily shake off negative experiences (much like any mammal that shimmies their body after a stressful encounter) and return to a *set point* that is shifting closer to serenity and contentment.

I sometimes even catch myself with a smile for absolutely no reason, such as in the middle of a practice session amid a busy mind and pain in my hip. A gentle smile creeps in that has nothing to do with what I'm doing. The negativity bias seems to be receding, and I'm better able to meet new situations and circumstances with more optimism and joy and bounce back from the more challenging ones with more ease.

Loving-kindness–based Practices

It's good to grow the good.

– Dr. Rick Hanson

If becoming aware of our immediate surroundings and sensory experience again and again over a short period can bring about such a favorable shift in our well-being, what would happen if we actively tried to cultivate positive experiences? Once we stop the pain (the digging), can what we do with our time and energy actually grow the good? Can we consciously cultivate more positivity for ourselves?

Loving-kindness practice, a specific exercise that focuses on wishing good things for ourselves and others, is one such way. Research shows it can generate more positive mood experiences and, it turns out, much more.

In a 2008 study, researcher Barbara Fredrickson and her team used loving-kindness meditation to test a hypothesis that positive daily experiences compounded over time create a variety of benefits, including increases in positive emotions, mindfulness, purpose in life, social support and a reduction in illness symptoms. The research confirmed these benefits and, moreover, that a loving-kindness practice in itself leads to increased life satisfaction and reduced depressive symptoms.[39]

Even more powerfully, in another study with nonmeditating migraine sufferers who were exposed to one twenty-minute guided loving-kindness meditation session, participants reported a 33 percent decrease in pain and a 43 percent decrease in emotional tension.[40] This study showed not only significant effectiveness but also the immediacy of this particular intervention for migraine headache sufferers.

These benefits also translate to persistent pain as noted in a 2005 study with chronic lower back pain sufferers exposed to an eight-week

[39] Fredrickson, B. L., Cohn, M. A., Coffey, K. A., Pek, J., & Finkel, S. M. (2008). Open hearts build lives: Positive emotions, induced through loving-kindness meditation, build consequential personal resources. *Journal of Personality and Social Psychology*, 95(5), 1045–1062. http://doi.org/10.1037/a0013262

[40] Tonelli, M. E., & Wachholtz, A. B. (2014). Meditation-based treatment yielding immediate relief for meditation-naïve migraineurs. *Pain Management Nursing*, 15(1), 36–40. http://doi.org/10.1016/j.pmn.2012.04.002

loving-kindness program.[41] In this study, analyses showed significant improvements in pain and psychological distress in the loving-kindness group but no changes in the control group who were given the usual care. What's more, analysis of daily data showed that more loving-kindness practice on a given day was related to lower pain that day and lower anger the next day.

The promise of using loving-kindness practice to treat PTSD was revealed in a study with veterans. Overall, the loving-kindness meditation was associated with reduced symptoms of PTSD and depression for the participants, even months after the twelve-week course ended.[42]

Loving-kindness practice decreases stress[43] and the decline of age-related biological markers.[44] It also increases empathy, compassion for self and others, helpfulness, and social connection and has been shown to decrease self-criticism.[45]

Given such minimal investment of time (as little as ten minutes a day) and the many payoffs reaped from this simple practice, it is

---

[41] Carson, J. W., Keefe, F. J., Lynch, T. R., Carson, K. M., Goli, V., Fras, A. M., & Thorp, S. R. (2005). Loving-kindness meditation for chronic low back pain: results from a pilot trial. *Journal of Holistic Nursing: Official Journal of the American Holistic Nurses' Association*, *23*(3), 287–304. http://doi.org/10.1177/0898010105277651

[42] Kearney, D. J., Malte, C. A., McManus, C., Martinez, M. E., Felleman, B., & Simpson, T. L. (2013). Loving-kindness meditation for posttraumatic stress disorder: A pilot study: Loving-kindness meditation for PTSD. *Journal of Traumatic Stress*, *26*(4), 426–434. http://doi.org/10.1002/jts.21832

[43] Law, W. M. R. (2011). An analogue study of loving-kindness meditation as a buffer against social stress. Retrieved from http://arizona.openrepository.com/arizona/handle/10150/145398

[44] Hoge, E. A., Chen, M. M., Orr, E., Metcalf, C. A., Fischer, L. E., Pollack, M. H., & Simon, N. M. (2013). Loving-kindness meditation practice associated with longer telomeres in women. *Brain, Behavior, and Immunity*, *32*, 159–163. http://doi.org/10.1016/j.bbi.2013.04.005

[45] Seppälä, E. (2014, October 1). 18 Science-based reasons to try loving-kindness meditation. Retrieved May 19, 2016, from http://www.mindful.org/18-science-based-reasons-to-try-loving-kindness-meditation/

hard to think of reasons *not* to take up a loving-kindness practice or a mindfulness practice.

And the beauty is it doesn't matter where we are. It doesn't matter where we start from. The benefits begin the moment we start and continue to resonate long after we stop, but why would we stop something that helps us feel so good in so many ways?

Intentional Living

Chapter 9

The Cradle of Creation

If you wish to make an apple pie from scratch, you must first invent the universe.

— *Carl Sagan, Cosmos*

I love this quote as a reminder that we exist in a larger *container, or field,* called the universe. Without it, we or anything we want or experience wouldn't exist. As I've engaged over the years with countless coaching clients who've arrived at my office with big aspirations, our work primarily focuses on creating the *conditions* necessary for their vision to emerge.

This involves an exciting journey of deep exploration to discover what is important to us and why. From this emerges an important vision we hold for ourselves. And as it turns out, the vision is usually inextricably intertwined with who we *are*—the very *essence* of our being—and includes our exquisitely unique combination of talents and abilities. When we work toward stepping into the resulting vision that arises from our work, we shift our focus to who we need to *be*.

What conditions of being allow this vision to manifest?

If my heartfelt vision includes bringing attention to the suffering that elephants are experiencing so that humans can be entertained, then I must *be* someone with enough *courage* to step out of my comfort zone to help shift a multigenerational and international practice of harm toward these majestic beings. (As it happens, this is a passion and pursuit of mine.)

But first things first, I need to bring into awareness these deeper callings. From discovering these truths, I can better align my heart, mind, and body and aim them in the same direction. We begin with simple questions, just allowing the answers to bubble up to the surface of our awareness.

Exercise: What Do I Like?

Use a piece of paper or set up an area of your journal and create three columns: "Loves," "No Preference" (or "Neutral"), and "Dislikes." Spend a week or so paying particular attention to what your senses like and dislike as well as those things that create no particular reaction. You can experiment by purposefully introducing things into your experience and test them or just notice what arises from your regular routine. (Both are valuable and reveal important truths about where you are and where you'd like to be.) Here are some things you can consider.

- What do the eyes enjoy seeing? What is hard for them to bear witness to? What forces them to close?
- What sounds bring a sense of calm, harmony, and peace in the body? What brings excitement? Irritation? Shutting down?

- What fragrances attract you? What ones cause your nose to close and turn away?
- What are some of your favorite tastes? What ones cause "yuck!" to spontaneously spew out of your mouth?
- What sensations delight you? Soft, tender caresses? Deep, penetrating massage? Long, slow stretches that bring you to the edge of comfort? The feel of your favorite clothing or hair brushing against your skin? What sensations make you recoil? Shiver? Turn away? Say "ouch!"?
- At the end of the week, reflect to see if you discovered something new about what attracts you. Also, what did you notice about the experiences that didn't move you one way or another—the neutral ones?

While these may seem very rudimentary—much like those a young child would notice when experiencing things for the first time—most of us come to realize from this exercise that we've lost connection with these very basic touch points of our life. Whether losing connection through the busyness of our lives or conditioning, when we actively consider them, we may remember that pleasure and discomfort actually rest in more simple experiences.

As our mindfulness deepens, we become more available for simple sensory exchanges to reach our awareness, potentially bringing more vividly rich, varied, and delight-filled experiences. If we are wanting a life of happiness as most do, discovering these basic experiences that bring peace and pleasure to our heart, mind, and body is a vital first step. We may rediscover the freshness and simple sensual enjoyment of eating a ripe, juicy peach or, conversely, notice our body recoil in reaction to loud, grating sounds.

Beginning with very basic self-exploration is an ideal first step to gain clarity of what can bring us more peace, contentment, and joy.

Dr. Rick Hanson, in his book *Hardwiring Happiness*, invites us to purposely rewire the negativity bias and "grow the good" through intentionally doing and thinking more positive things. As we do, he recommends to mindfully and purposefully become more conscious as these good things are happening as a way to rewire the neural networks in the brain. Over time, this will replace our automatic tendency to focus on the negative and experience more good.

Thanks to recent findings in neuroscience, we're learning that not only do we contribute to creating our own reality by how and what we think in the moment of our experience, but our thoughts and actions in that moment actually also change our biology and physiology. The shift in physiology changes our future experiences as we've learned with the studies on mindfulness and loving-kindness. Or as Dr. Hanson puts it, "We can change our mind to change our brain to change our mind." And so on. This is one way that we can actively cocreate a more positive future for ourselves.

I can remember being scoffed at in my early twenties when I shared that I believed we created our own reality. It was the early 1980s when affirmations were all the rage in the New Age movement. And while it made sense to me—"As a man thinketh, so he is"—others in my circle of friends considered it childish and foolish.

This reaction fostered an earnest quest to discover the truth that spanned inward and outward through spiritual traditions and scientific discovery. What was true at the macro as well as the micro level? What was at the forefront of scientific knowledge? What did ancient texts reveal about the deeper truths of life? What did my own experience tell me?

A captivating portion of this search took me to the field of quantum physics, particularly through the work of Fritjof Capra in *The Tao of Physics*. It was here where I felt I found sufficient proof (for my young mind at the time) that we literally create our own reality. Today

I understand more clearly that while we don't control or have the sole power in creation, we are, in fact, a vital and integral part of the seemingly ceaseless unfolding process of creation.

Because of our consciousness, we are cocreators.

Neuroscience confirms this connection. As we deepen our conscious connection with our experience, our awareness itself changes our experience; it deepens, broadens, and becomes more vivid, which changes our brain's physiology. The brain's ability to reorganize itself by forming new neural connections, called *neuroplasticity,* is how we can consciously "grow our good."

As an aside, the exploration to discover these deeper truths has held the most meaning for me in life—that and experiencing healthy relationship and love. It's what I do and who I am at the same time, and when I'm outside of this exploration, I have a tendency to get lost in the mundane, experiencing a lot of discomfort through lack of deeper meaning, purpose, and contribution in life.

But getting back to Hanson's invitation to grow the good through really focusing on consciously absorbing—drinking in—our positive experiences, neuroscientists have confirmed that the longer something is held in awareness and the more emotionally stimulating it is, the more neurons fire. Every experience, thought, feeling, and physical sensation ignites thousands of neurons, forming what are known as *neural networks.* When you repeat an experience over and over, the brain learns to fire the same neurons each time with a quicker response time, and well-worn pathways are developed.

So as we discussed earlier regarding the body's automatic response to threat because those neural networks are so deeply embedded and wired together, even though our lives are not in immediate jeopardy, overcoming that instinct takes a *lot* of consciousness in the moment to reassure us we are not in danger.

The same can be true for those who experienced major traumas. For instance, if we've been harmed through touch in a dramatic way, that will hardwire in our brains. And when someone reaches out to touch us with a kind intention, we may still feel our skin crawl. Or if we've experienced the ravages of war—excessively loud blasts, witnessing harm and destruction—anytime an experience faintly resembles the situation, we may find ourselves triggered back into the same biological response that occurred then.

Reorienting out of the dominance of the negativity bias or trauma takes time and repetition. Patience and compassion are needed, but the process of gradually "rewiring" the brain is an assured one.

So, we can work growing joy in our lives in at least two ways—waking up to nonthreatening experiences when our body has gone into fight, flight, or freeze mode; and consciously directing our efforts and attention toward creating more positive experiences. The thing I find most fascinating is that while there are so many things beyond our control, we still contribute a great deal to the outcome of situations through our conscious intention and actions.

We are partners in cocreating our lives and experiences.

What No Longer Serves Me?

We can trust our growing self-love and awareness to burn through layers of conditioning and reveal more of our authentic nature and values.

Mindfulness helps calm the mind, allowing opportunity for a uniquely rich and thoughtful inward gaze toward our precious life to emerge. But as our gaze rotates toward this sumptuous inner life, we may, at first, be bombarded with a conglomeration of stories, feelings, and judgments arising from an unexamined life, namely, layers upon layers of unconscious conditioning accumulated over a lifetime.

So deeply embedded in our being is this conditioning, we may never know, much less question, the values, beliefs, and assumptions that underlie most of our inner world and most of our decisions. But as our awareness grows and we tease apart these previously unexamined layers with the light of loving awareness, we are also given the opportunity to question whether they actually serve to reduce pain and suffering and welcome in more pleasure, joy, and happiness.

With a deeper and heartfelt look, though, the convictions we've lived our life by may be quite startling or disturbing. At these times, remembering our greater intention to meet ourselves and our experience with a gentle, loving acceptance and kindness can be a wise approach to meeting potentially undesirable elements of our thoughts, beliefs, and values.

These deeper inquiries may bring to light how we've been living out of integrity with our most cherished values. It's important to be sympathetic and tender with ourselves as we take steps to stop "digging the hole." Cultivating a *willingness* to let go of these ways of being that no longer serve us offers us new hope. Bringing compassionate awareness helps us let go more easily.

> *We can't force ourselves to let go. Letting go is a byproduct of awareness.*
>
> *— Sharda Rogell*

As we turn our attention inward, the crazy-making frantic thoughts darting here and there begin to subside, making way for the mysteriously sublime *divine whisper*. As we become more attuned to it, we can learn to participate in a dance of cocreation, bringing our direction and actions into appreciable alignment with the truth of our being. Through setting our compass's direction and regularly affirming that direction with thoughts, words, and deeds, we undertake a journey to fulfill our deeper purpose and passion—a journey of potentially profound proportions.

Thoughts as Creative Force

> *Imagination is everything. It is the preview*
> *of life's coming attractions.*
>
> —*Albert Einstein*

If you look around at this very moment, virtually every human-made object you see, someone, somewhere had some form of *thought* (image, words, story, etc.) about it prior to creating it. With the possible exception of an improvisational artistic expression not anchored in prior thought, whether they are conscious or not, thoughts come prior to seeing an object in form.

If what is around you right now is mostly nature, you can settle with the idea of the ongoing generative forces of nature at work—seeds formed and dropped; birds, through their process of eating, casting them to new places; sprouts popping up after the first rains, etc. Similar to your birth, conscious or not, your parents took actions, and you were conceived. While we don't know all the details of how a tiny human is formed, when we make love, this action is a catalyst of creation.

Setting our thoughts toward our goals and vision not only increases our chances of success but also begins a mysterious process of creation. And as we can't know the unknowable details and steps to birthing a baby, we can't know all the details and steps to birthing our goals and vision. But we plant the seed within our hearts and through our thoughts.

> *Once you make a decision, the Universe*
> *conspires to make it happen.*
>
> —*Ralph Waldo Emerson*

Our success is amplified when our thoughts are aligned with our heartfelt vision, not only because we are more aware of and attuned to them regularly but also because we are more present in the moment to take advantage of synchronistic opportunities.

Planting thought seeds and affirming your intentions sets your trajectory toward your goals, and greater success and happiness are available if you move from a place of intention rather than expectation.

Chapter 10

Intention versus Expectation

Expectation is the root of all heartache.

—William Shakespeare

Understanding the difference between intention and expectation will make a world of difference as you journey toward your goals. Living life from expectation creates enormous amounts of unnecessary suffering.

Living from *intention* situates us in the present moment, moving forward toward our intended destination. Basically, intention gives awareness direction. When we live from intention, we are grounded in our body, our attention is with us and our experience, and we are filled with purposeful direction. Our energy is open and engaged with the unfolding flow of the moment.

Intention gives awareness direction.

Alternatively, with *expectation*, we usually have a very specific and narrowly defined *outcome* in our mind's eye. With more narrowly focused attention, we put very little attention on our direct experience.

Sometimes obsessed, living from expectation can blind us to the life before us, missing out not only on the only opportunity we have to experience this moment but also on potential opportunistic connections and avenues toward our larger, overarching goal—our vision for our self and our life.

For instance, if I'm looking for a new home, I may picture it with great detail: a 1,500 square foot home in a quiet neighborhood, with two bedrooms and two bathrooms. I may see it painted white with a large fenced yard for my dog.

I may fantasize about a claw-foot tub in a bright and sunny location with big windows. Being clear on what I want is an important step in setting intention, but if I define it too narrowly, I spend most of my time comparing that vision to the homes I see. I mostly see how they don't measure up. I will most likely spend a lot of time in disappointment with approaching my vision and goals from expectation. If I keep a too narrowly defined vision, there are fewer opportunities for my needs and desires to get met.

We may think that taking time to get specific about our vision means filling in all the exact details and launching headlong straight toward it, but the specificity needed to cocreate a life we love is more about distilling our vision to the very essence of what we'll receive when we reach it than it is about choosing colors, size, and location.

> *An intention is simply a thought impulse which gives structure and direction to creative energy. It arises from a neutral state of awareness. Expectation is a hope that something will happen. It comes from an ego state that is identified or attached to the outcome. Using intention allows you to remain detached from the outcome.*
>
> *— Deepak Chopra*

One of the clearest examples I know of moving toward a vision from a place of intention was in the case of my current home. When it was getting clear I was no longer able to secure enough firewood for the winter on my strength alone, and as Shyla aged, at some point she wouldn't be able to walk the quarter mile to our front doorstep, the reality of our situation sparked the calling to find a new home. It was time to move from the remotely located single room cabin we'd lived in for almost a decade.

Living and discovering the sheer delight of voluntary simplicity for so long, there weren't too many things that I considered necessary. I had found exceptional peace and joy in needing very little. While I wanted to retain the simplicity of our lives, I also wanted to make sure we had the basic necessities met—the primary being easy access to our home.

I was also ready to free up my time from the daily chores of living so I could focus on other work. In addition to chainsawing, hauling, and splitting all the firewood, we didn't have indoor plumbing or running water. Two-gallon outdoor showers or dishwashing with water heated on the stove, while thoroughly enjoyable, took time. Cooking and drinking water, five-gallon tanks of propane, and an occasional heavy auto battery that was part of the solar system were pushed up and down the sometimes slippery and mucky, sometimes dry and dusty hill in a wheelbarrow. This was in addition to the groceries, laundry, and garbage carted up and down the hill regularly. It was time to move.

I had in my heart the ideal general area I wanted to live but wanted to also stay open to what the universe may have in store for me next. I spent time over the next few months pondering more about what would really nourish and fulfill me.

That process kept returning me to the biggest drivers at the time, making sure Shyla's final years were comfortable, freeing up time for other interests, and making day-to-day life easier while staying affordable. Given these basic requirements, there would be myriad possibilities for our new home.

Moving from this intention, I was clear what I wanted but had no idea what it was going to look like. I had to stay present in the moment, seeing and tuning into what was here and calmly assessing it. Because I wasn't caught looking for a lot of specific details, I was actively engaging in an open-ended process.

> *The other thing I was sure of—if I retained present-moment awareness, I would know and feel it when I saw it. I would be in touch with my deep "yes."*

The process of finding our new home took about a year and a half, with more than a few frustrating possibilities coming together and falling apart. In fact, it wasn't until I had pretty much given up on being able to buy a home and instead looked at rentals that my home manifested. I thought for sure something would have manifested and became willing to settle for something less than ideal because I knew for sure I wasn't spending another winter in the cabin.

In the end, thanks to help from friends, a home that far exceeded my intention found me. Shyla lived out her days in comfort, and I continue to be nourished inside and out with unimaginable beauty, comfort, and ease. I am grateful daily for this home that is far grander and more perfect for me than my conscious thoughts and dreams held. And I never would have seen it had I operated from expectation.

An attitude of expectation is sometimes tricky to notice. I usually discover it when I find myself smacking up against some difficulty repeatedly or at a closed door. When this happens, if I ask myself, "What is my expectation here?" I can tell from the answer if I've fallen into expectation.

This bitter trap can really sneak up on me in my relationships, particularly with loved ones. Sometimes when taking a romantic getaway weekend, an anniversary, or other holiday celebration, my expectations around what I think these events should be inevitably create pain for myself and my partner, particularly if I'm operating off the assumption that my partner has the same vision and ideals for our adventure.

We can still bring great energy to manifesting from intention, but loosening our attachment to the outcome may not only lead to better results, we'll more likely enjoy the creative process along the way. Rather than spending our journey nervous or anxious about reaching our destination, we can use the opportunity to deepen our sense of play and joyful engagement.

> *We can give our best to the process, create what we can and trust the larger process of life itself. We can plan, we can care for, tend and respond. But we cannot control.*

> *— Jack Kornfield*

We may have discovered already that our thoughts are filled with expectations. Sometimes expectations are built out of beliefs and values of how we and others *should* behave and act, and sometimes they are built around *entitlements*—that it's our right or privilege to have something. Through loving inquiry, we can untangle and tease apart how these expectations have been operating in our lives. In doing so, we may discover a new freedom and a new way of being in the world, one that trusts in a more loving and caring unfolding that includes our greatest good.

Exercise: Does Operating from Expectations Serve Me?

Reflect in your journal about events in your life where you were really wanting something specific and didn't receive it. Were you operating from expectation? If so, upon reflection, were you blinded and unable to be with and enjoy the journey? What was brought to you instead? How did you receive it when it arrived?

Further reflect, what is the general tendency when you have an expectation? Is there a pattern? Is living expectantly serving you? If not, are you willing to let it go and open to something different?

Chapter 11

What Do Beliefs and Values Have to Do with Happiness?

A highly developed values system is like a compass. It serves as a guide to point you in the right direction when you are lost.

— Idowu Koyenikan

Most of us move through our lives, making decisions based on beliefs and values that are usually unconscious. They are so much an undercurrent, we sometimes even assume that they are shared by everyone. Beliefs and values can play a role in creating expectations, leading us from frustration to potential agony as we witness others living differently that we think they should. We may think that our beliefs and values are inherent in our being, just a part of truth that everyone should hold. But really, they aren't.

Beliefs and values are learned and chosen.

Though sometimes deeply rooted and hard to discern, this recognition can lead to greater freedom, choice, and meaning in our lives. Take a moment to recall a belief or value you had in youth that you no longer believe. Was it Santa Claus? The tooth fairy? Or one of the many fantasy stories we as children held to be true until we learned differently?

With this reflection, it's easy to see how beliefs are learned and chosen and, even more, how they affect our behavior. I know I was always better behaved as the holidays approached, hoping Santa would see me in *those* moments.

Beliefs that are deeply ingrained in our formative years are usually the most difficult to distinguish as chosen because we most likely adopted them seamlessly from our families, educational system, and/or the dominant culture of our youth.

Racism and sexism were so deeply ingrained in the early 1960s rural America of my youth. I couldn't help but adopt those beliefs and values; they were so invisibly woven into every level of my world. I still can hear echoes of harsh judgments in my mind, but thanks to my growing mindfulness, I no longer automatically take action on these thoughts. The spaciousness between thought and response allows discernment and wisdom to guide my actions more and more.

While mindfulness practices help increase our ability to accept and allow things as they are, we also grow in the capacity to change our conditioned habits, beliefs, and values when we unearth an inner conflict. I certainly no longer consciously hold the beliefs surrounding these divisive values; they have been replaced over the years with new information from education and my own experiences.

I find it fascinating to be simultaneously learning about my long-held beliefs and adopted values, letting go of ones that no longer serve me, and adopting new views and standards that resonate more deeply with my emerging heartfelt self and aspirations. While the process can sometimes be momentarily dissonant as today's chosen values clash with those of the past, I work to ensure my compassionate container is strong enough for the process itself.

Exercise: Deeply Held Beliefs and Values

Reflect in your journal on the different beliefs you held as a child that you know today to not be true.

Next, take a look at your values. What early values did you give up? Why? Which ones do you continue to live with that really don't resonate or serve you? Are you willing to release them? How does that feel?

Finding Peace and Freedom Through Practice

While mindfulness of breath will bring many benefits during and outside of practice, gathering and focusing our attention is only the beginning stage of a mindfulness practice. Ideally, we want to bring our loving attention to all our life experiences. The following chapters will guide you through the differing realms of experience.

Chapter 12

Coming to Our Senses

Realize that this very body, with its aches and its pleasures . . . is exactly what we need to be fully human, fully awake, fully alive.

— *Pema Chodron*

At this point, we may have discovered many subtleties about our breath: its tendency to slow down and settle into a rhythm when our mind and body are at rest; its susceptibility to change when emotionally charged thoughts arise; or its habit to even, on occasion, stop for a period. The breath is a primary focusing factor, but it is much more; it is our first portal to our moment by moment lived experience in our body. We're now ready to expand our attentional field of awareness to include our *five senses*—sight, sound, touch, smell, and taste.

In learning to accept and allow the breath to be as it is, to become participant witnesses, we are training to meet our other *experiences*—the conditions of how things are—as they are.

Additionally, following the natural breath wakens us to a deeper truth: everything is in motion; nothing is fixed. There is no final experience; it's a continual flow. Working with the senses will help us experience this even more fully.

We most likely have also discovered what a busy mind we have. I offer you assurance that you are not alone. When we stop and see the busy mind for the first time, we may think this is about us and the circumstances of our lives, but really, it isn't. It is about the nature of the mind. Just as the nature of the eyes are to see, the ears to hear, and the heart to beat, the mind thinks. That's its job, and we wouldn't be anywhere without it.

With the ever-wandering mind, a lot of our practice becomes an exercise in just returning to this moment again and again. And since the mind's main job is to work for our greater good, rather than judging ourselves when the mind has wandered off, we can instead rejoice that the mind is still working away for our benefit.

For now, as we continue to build our mindfulness muscle, we are still not concerned with the details of where the mind wanders, what story it's spinning, or how long it has been gone. With peaceful equanimity, we simply pick our attention and place it back on the breath again and again. It is like training a playful and squirming puppy—we use a kind, firm, and patient persistence.

In the next phase of exploration, as we learn how to expand our field of loving awareness to include our physical senses, a new richness and aliveness awakens through our sense doors—those areas of our body that meet the outside world. These are the very instruments we use to engage in the world and the very place we experience the things we most want in our lives—love, joy, meaning, happiness, etc. Developing an intimate relationship with our senses is the doorway to the good in our lives. It is where the rubber meets the road.

They are, of course, the same places that we experience deep, sometimes wrenching pain. But as we'll soon discover, these difficult emotional states themselves are shifting and changing waves of sensations too. Pain actually becomes more bearable when we can be present and attend to it with loving, tender awareness rather than tightening down to resist it.

*We can't shut out the bad without compromising
our ability to experience the good.*

In essence, we use sensory awareness exercises as a way to further befriend our bodies and our heart's longing.

The Invitation

The moment one gives close attention to anything, even a blade of grass, it becomes a mysterious, awesome, indescribably magnificent world in itself.

— Henry Miller

Some sensory meditation practices are designed to bring a more expansive, broad, and inclusive experience, while others are more focused, offering a path to greater flexibility and potential relief from pains in the body. We can use our growing intuition to help guide us towards which practice to use based on our needs at the time.

Here's a basic practice that can help you arrive more fully in your body in the moment. It can serve as a general pathway to either the expansive or focused practice.

Practice: Opening the Sense Doors

This seated practice helps us gain an awakened sense in the body. Allow yourself fifteen to twenty minutes for this exploration. Find a comfortable seated position that allows for ease and alertness.

With the excited interest of a kindergartener on their first safari, look around the area you're seated. A kindergartener would be seeing all this for the first time, so they might begin by looking at the outline and shape of the animals they see. They may notice how big or small they are. They might bring a particular attentiveness to the colors, noticing shades and brightness.

As your eyes settle into the space, new things may come into your awareness, such as textures and patterns. Explore these. Next, shift your attention to include noticing light and how the presence or absence of light brings a depth and dimension to the objects you see. Stay curious. What more is revealed as you look around?

Next, notice the quality of movement in what you see. Sometimes movement is actually happening; other times there is a sense of movement built into a stationary object. What do you notice? Finally, look at the spaces between objects. What happens to your perception?

Keeping your sight engaged, slowly and gently close your eyes, and continue looking for the same qualities and characteristics you did with eyes open: shapes, colors, patterns, textures, light, shadow, and movement. With your eyes closed, you may not see distinct shapes and sizes, but you may visually discern more patterns and textures. Colors may not be so vivid, but movement and patterns may be more so. Again, just notice what arises in the field of sight with an interested attention.

After a few moments, shift your attention to the sounds around you, and begin a discovery of their characteristics as a five-year-old private detective would. Are they loud? Soft? Are they persistent, or is there a beginning and end to them? Are they distant or near? Are they sharp or dull? Nature-made or machine-made? Spend some time tuning into the sounds themselves and their nature with the same curiosity you did with seeing objects.

Next, turn your attention to any fragrances you can detect and explore their essential qualities. Strong? Soft? Sweet? Sharp? Pungent? Do the same for the tastes in the mouth. Can you detect any? If so, are they strong? Sweet? Sour? Bitter? Salty?

Next, bring your curious attention to the physical essence of your body. Begin with the characteristic of weight and notice how your body is being received by earth through your chair or cushion. Notice how gravity is doing most of the work.

Next, notice the touch points where the body meets a surface. Are they hard or soft? How dense is the connection? Is the surface cushiony? How about where your hands are resting or where your feet meet the floor? What do you experience there?

Further tuning into the body, see if you can notice temperature. Maybe the heart, torso, and hands have a sense of warmth, and where the skin is exposed there is a sense of coolness. How about the feet? Whatever is occurring, just meet it directly, without overlaying any "shoulds" or judgments. Just allow your awareness to meet what is present. If you notice yourself judging what you're experiencing, notice that and try to refrain from judging the judging and just return to the exercise.

Next, sweep your attention from the crown of the head toward the feet and explore the sensation on the surface of your skin. Maybe it's clothing, or your hair or just the air. Is the texture soft? Rough? Smooth? Silky? Thick? Dense? Do you notice movement of the texture running across the skin? How about your hair? Can you feel it touching gently on your skin? Can you feel the very bottom of your feet?

Sweep your curious attention back from the feet upward toward the head, this time tuning into the movement in the body, most likely from breathing. Maybe you feel your belly expand and contract, possibly experiencing a tension and release at your waistband. Or maybe you can feel the rise and fall of the shoulders and chest area as the breath fills and leaves the lungs. Perhaps you can feel the swirling and tingling movement of the air at the entrance of the nostrils as it is being pulled into the lungs. Maybe you can feel the air brush across the upper lip, move the hairs inside the nose, or turn the corner down the windpipe.

Staying with the sense of movement in the body for a period, choose one of the following ways to continue the practice:

Practice: Exploring Senses with the Breath as Anchor

(This is a good body-based practice to use when you are feeling scattered and/or anxious and want to strengthen your focus and attention.)

Anchor your attention to the breath for a brief period of time. Then, whenever a sensation or other sensory experience (sounds, smells, etc.) competes with your attention to the breath, allow your awareness to go fully to it, exploring for as long as it is present or until you are at ease with it. Then return to the breath, staying anchored there until the next sense experience vies for your attention.

If you find your mind wandering, note that the mind is thinking, and anchor your attention back to the breath, without judgment.

Practice: Choiceless (or Spacious) Awareness

(This is an effective practice for helping us let go when we are holding on too tightly either in our body or to a situation.)

After opening the sense doors individually as above, allow your attention to become broad, including all the senses and sensations at once with an expansive, inclusive attention. Allow the field of awareness to expand out of the body and fill the space where you are. Continue growing the awareness until it is as big as the immeasurable blue sky that allows all the weather to come and go as it will but remains steady, unaffected, and clear blue.

With a vast and allowing awareness, experience the waves of sensation manifest and dissipate. Practice remaining spacious and unattached to what arises in your whole field of awareness, and as the mind wanders, as it will, note it as just another cloud forming and dissipating in the empty spaciousness of the ever-expanding sky.

Practice: The Body Scan

(This practice serves as a loving, caring way to gain mastery over placing our attention. A tremendously helpful shift can occur for perceiving and relating to difficult sensations. It also strengthens concentration and flexibility.)

Comfortably lying on your back with eyes closed, collect your attention to the breath for a few minutes. Next, place your attention on the big toe of the left foot. Rest it there for a few breaths, just experiencing and noting whatever sensations are present. Maybe you can feel the pressure and sensation of covers or a sock. Give yourself a few moments of focused attention to see what you feel. Then move your attention to the rest of the toes, and spend a few breaths there experiencing whatever there is to notice.

If you can't detect any sensation after a few breaths, then accepting that as the experience, gently move on. Conversely, if the sensation is intense, either pleasant or unpleasant, just stay present with a loving and accepting attention for the few breaths and move on.

Direct your attention systematically around in the body: left toes to foot, to ankle, to calf, to knee, to thigh. Then move to the right toes, to right foot, to ankle, to calf, to knee, to thigh, to pelvic region. Move up from the pelvic region to the belly and lower back. Next, spend a few breaths on the upper chest and upper back region, again just noticing what sensations arise.

Now, move your attention down to the fingers on the left hand and work your way up to the shoulder. Spend a few breaths in each section then switch to the fingers on the right and sweep your attention up. From the shoulder area, move to the neck, the back of the head and then the face.

Once complete, you can explore by bringing attention to the whole body by either sweeping broad strokes up and down the body or keeping attention attuned to the whole body all at once. Play with this, and alternate back and forth from the section by section practice to the broader, more inclusive practice.

One of the difficulties with practicing the body scan in a supine position is, naturally, falling asleep. This can be a telltale sign of tiredness or exhaustion and should be met with kindness and acceptance. You can either use this as an exercise of bringing alertness and brightness to your attention through noting the sleepiness, or if you are having difficulty sleeping, use this as an exercise to help you fall asleep.

If you live with acute chronic pain, the exercise may be challenging at first to keep the attention moving and not settling onto an area of pain. Because of the systematic application of awareness, this practice helps us learn how to accept and allow the difficult and painful sensations while not ignoring them, receiving them lovingly and kindly but not focusing all our attention on them.

We work to give equal time to the painful areas just as we do the other areas of our body. This helps retrain the negativity bias in the brain, which wants to focus only on the difficult. It also strengthens our ability to find the good in our body and in our lives, even when we are experiencing persistent difficulty.

Because of the tendency to help the mind gain stability, calmness, and awareness, using a variation of the body scan can be particularly valuable for those managing chronic pain. An additional supportive practice of breathing an intentional breath of kindness into an area of pain may create a shift in sensation. While it is important not to strive for any particular outcome with the breath, the exploration into what does occur may create benefit in itself. The invitation is to see what you experience as you practice the variation, always maintaining a sense of peaceful allowance of your experience while fostering a spacious awareness of what you meet. This in itself is known to help ease discomfort.

Learning to work with pain in an accepting and compassionate way takes time and patience, but the benefits are certainly worth it. One of my students who suffers from *fibromyalgia*—a disorder with widespread musculoskeletal pain that includes fatigue, sleep, memory, and mood issues—was able to stay still for longer periods with less pain as a result of this and other mindfulness practices.[46]

Another area to bring our fuller attention to for countless benefits is our eating. Food is the basic fuel for our bodies. We can treat how we get our energy like how we fill up our gas tank—a quick dash to the filling station—or we can turn it into a sumptuous and pleasant experience, even if we're in a hurry.

---

[46] For a comprehensive exploration of the body scan and working with pain, see Jon Kabat-Zinn's *Full Catastrophe Living*.

Practice: Bringing Joy Back to Food

Start with a small piece of food, maybe a strawberry, raisin, or pea. Placing it in your palm, invite in a childlike quality of curiosity as if you've never seen this type of food before. Notice its shape and color, its texture and size. Roll it around in your hand. Notice how you respond to it. Does a smile show up?

Take a few moments to reflect on all the people and steps that were needed for this morsel to end up in your hand—from the farmers that planted and tended the seeds to the rain and sunshine needed and the field workers that harvested it. From the packers and truckers that moved it to the store to the store clerks that put it on the shelf. From the checkers where you purchased it to you or whoever brought it home and prepared it. Offer a bit of gratitude to each who participated.

Closing your eyes, notice its weight and feel in your palm. Bring it close to your nose, and take a good long whiff, noticing not only the fragrance but also how your body responds to it. Does your mouth water? (Saliva begins our digestive process. If we skip this important part, it's harder on the body.)

Next, place it in your mouth, and let it rest on your tongue. Can you detect its flavor? Notice how the mouth responds. More saliva? Feel the texture and shape with your tongue. Roll it around in your mouth if you'd like. Then slowly bite down. What happens? As you begin chewing, notice what happens with the flavor and texture. When you swallow, see how far your awareness can follow it down. Can you feel it move into the stomach? How long does the flavor last in your mouth? Where does it go?

For the formal practice, using one small piece of food is best, but adapting this approach for everyday eating is encouraged. If you enjoy the pleasurable flavors of food, sitting with the lingering flavor between bites prolongs the pleasure you receive. We tend to eat less the slower we eat, as the brain and body have time to register the food, and we tend to receive more enjoyment.

Each of these sensory practices can amplify our awareness while grounding it more fully into our body. It can also awaken us to areas and sensations that we may never have experienced before, or haven't for a very long time. Mindfulness of our senses increases our capacity to notice difficulties with an attitude of kindness and acceptance as well as enjoy pleasant sensations more fully.

Grounding our awareness in the body is a crucial part of the feedback loop needed to stay healthy, cocreate a life of meaning and value for ourselves, learn to lovingly navigate through pain, and, most importantly, to experience our life more fully. The latter allows us to reap the rewards of a life well lived.

Life requires you to be present to win.

Chapter 13

Mindfully Engaging with Thoughts

Do you have the patience to wait till your
mud settles and the water is clear? Can you remain
unmoving till the right action arises by itself?

— *Lao-Tzu, Tao te Ching*

We purposefully set aside thoughts while we learned to gather and steady our attention. The next two chapters bring the richly woven tapestry of thoughts and emotions into our growing field of awareness. Teasing apart the many-colored strands without getting tangled takes a refined awareness. We've prepared for this through the initial focusing and training of our attention.

The practice of noticing our thinking creates a growing spaciousness in our awareness, maybe enough so to recognize we are not our thoughts. Thoughts are objects that arise in awareness much like sounds, sights, and tastes.

The conscious experience of the "thinker" or "knower" — that part of ourselves that receives and interprets thoughts — creates a profound shift in relationship to and experience of those thoughts.

Like the breath, we can intentionally think a thought. Also like the breath, when we aren't consciously thinking a thought, the mind still generates them. Just as the body breathes without our attention or conscious action to create it, the mind produces thoughts without our attending to it. What a radical truth to come face-to-face with. We can and can't control these aspects of "*our*" being.

While we can cultivate conditions that help quiet the mind (focused attention, stillness, etc.) the mind stays pretty busy most of the time doing what it does best—think. We may have noticed that like a monkey running amok and wreaking havoc in the jungle, our mind is ultimately beyond our control.

Much as we'd like, we can't ultimately control our thinking.

Not recognizing this simple truth can create an incredibly painful *inner war* as we wrestle time and again, trying to put the mind in its place—to *cage the monkey* as it were. (If you haven't noticed this as a result of your practices thus far, don't take my word for it. I invite you to try to stop thinking for one simple minute.)

The mind may be beyond our control but it is not beyond our influence, and that's important to realize. We can cultivate conditions where the mind is more open to our *influence* and then guide it in a direction that is more meaningful for us.

From a mindfulness practice perspective, the invitation is to *end the inner war*—to accept the monkey as a monkey and not expect it to be, nor try to force it to be, a three-toed sloth.

How do we do this? By shifting our relationship with our mind and thoughts; by allowing thoughts to become just another object to observe in our field of awareness. Like a monkey running amok, we can learn to watch from a distance, maybe with growing amusement, the many tricks, ploys, tactics, and schemes it plays out.

*We can unhook ourselves and our awareness from
the thinking mind.*

Thoughts arise and pass in the same field of awareness that our breath and sensations arise in. So we approach them with the same engaged and open curiosity we do with the breath and sensations. By just allowing them to arise, unhindered, we explore them as would a monkey at the zoo.

Here are few ways to get started exploring thoughts.

Exercise: Counting Thoughts

Set a timer for three minutes, and collect your attention to either your breath, sounds, or sensations. When you notice a thought, keep count. At the end of the three minutes, notice how many thoughts arose. How busy was the mind today? Was it a monkey or a sloth? Try this exercise again at a different time of day and see what you notice.

From here, we can shift our exploration to see just what type of thoughts the mind is conjuring. If yours is anything like mine, there is a lot of planning, reflecting, figuring-it-out, judging, wanting, and pushing away going on. It is like a never-ending litany of judgments, scenarios, and requests.

Practice: Softly Noting Thoughts

Set your timer for ten minutes. Spend a few moments gathering your attention to the breath, sensations, or a combination that helps you anchor in the present. When you notice a thought arise, without judgment, try to categorize it softly in the background.

Maybe a thought arises about what you have planned for the day. You can internally note, "Planning, planning." The next thought may be something about how strange it is to be looking directly at your thoughts, so you softly note, "Judging, judging." If you can't categorize the thought easily, just note, "Thinking, thinking." After each thought subsides, return to your anchor.

When finished, take a few moments to reflect and inquire: What happened to your relationship with the thoughts in your field of awareness as you noted them? Did they soften? Did they disappear? What are the most reoccurring categories of thoughts you noticed?

Another valuable practice with thoughts, particularly emotionally charged ones, is to see how they show up in our body as sensations.

Exercise: What Does a Thought Feel Like?

Set a timer for ten minutes. Sit graciously and comfortably. Collect your attention with your chosen anchor—either the breath, sensation, sound, or combination. When a thought arises, shift your attention into the body to see where you feel it most. Experience and observe the actual sensations where they show up, without resistance or judgment. Notice how long the thought lasts and how long the sensations linger after the thought dissipates.

Get curious noticing what types of thoughts show up in similar parts of the body. How do the sensations differ? Where do pleasant thoughts show up? In the heart area? The face as a smile? How about unpleasant thoughts?

As we work more directly with thoughts, it's important to remember that we are not trying to generate or restrict thoughts but rather engage with interest the thoughts that arise in the mind without our effort, like with the natural breath. Thoughts that include a reference to "I," "me," or "mine" tend to have more of an emotional charge, showing up in stronger sensations in the body. Are you as readily able to simply note those as thoughts arising and passing away as you are with other thoughts?

Persistent Visitors, Inner Critic, and Core Beliefs

When thought is not looked at directly it can create a very convincing story. But when it is seen as the phenomenon that it is—just like a sound or sensation—the story falls apart.

— Unknown

As you turn more fully toward thoughts, you may begin to notice some *"persistent visitors"*—recurring thoughts, images, and stories that return frequently. *Welcome to the human condition!* In the mindfulness field, these are lovingly referred to as our *top ten hits*. (And they sometimes do show up as songs!) Learning to work with these persistent visitors with a little spacious sense of humor, acceptance, and patience can go a long way for our practice and reducing anxiety.

Sometimes our top ten hits will include various harsh judgments, usually about ourselves. Recognizing these can lead us to what's commonly known as our *inner critic*—that nitpicky inner voice that seems to sit on our shoulder and have something to say about everything we say and do.

Learning to work effectively with the inner critic can release us from the pain of that persistent voice of disapproving judgment—the one always at the ready to tell us how terribly we've messed up (once again) and how that makes us *unworthy as human beings*.

A favorite meditation teacher of mine, Mark Coleman, works extensively to help us release the agonizing grip of the inner critic. In *Make Peace with Your Mind: How Mindfulness and Compassion Can Free You from Your Inner Critic*, Coleman brings to life the excruciating suffering that arises from believing these disparaging stories about ourselves. He also guides us through wise, compassionate, and sometimes lighthearted and fun approaches to curb the tortuous fault finder.

You can usually tell when the inner critic is at work when you hear statements about you and your *value* as a human rather than a particular incident. "What an idiot! You're *always* late! Why can't you *ever* be on time? You are such a *schmuck*!" The inner critic is usually shame-based when it spews its harsh judgments.

There are many techniques to work with the inner critic to help lessen the damage this inner voice can have on our self-esteem, experience, and well-being. One of the most effective approaches I've learned is through observing and softly noting. This simple but powerful technique can help create a slight distance from the judgments, giving us an opportunity to better evaluate the assertions.

Using humor, sarcasm, or exaggeration with our inner critic is another way to break the hold and identification with serious judgments. "Oh, of course! I'm sure I'm the *only* person who's ever been late to a meeting, and there will *never* be another person late to a meeting. I am just an *incredible* louse!"

With the roominess in awareness that a mindfulness practice builds, we can actively question the statements we hear. Byron Katie has developed a powerful approach around questioning the truth of our thoughts called *The Work*. With this approach, as an assertion arises, we can note that the thought has arisen—this much is true—and then question the accuracy of the thought. Is it true? As we do, we may discover the opinion to be as untrue as the idea of purple polka-dotted giraffes.

Recently, when I was late to an important meeting, I lovingly questioned each statement the inner critic hurled my way:

"What an idiot!" Is that true? Well, in general, no. In general, I'm intelligent.

"You're always late!" Is that true? If so, then maybe I need to change something in my scheduling to remedy that. Not a big deal. If it's not true, if I'm not always late, then the validity of the statement is false.

The same is true for the next statement, "Why can't you *ever* be on time?" Well, I'm not always late, which means sometimes I'm on time—if only on occasion.

"You are such a schmuck!" Whether I'm always late or not doesn't determine my "*schmuckedness*." And this is where the most damage to my self-esteem can occur and also tells me this is the inner critic at play; my value as a human being is in question. It's gotten personal. It's name-calling. It's transcending the principle—being late—and landing in the personal.

This line of inquiry itself shifts my relationship with my thoughts *and* the inner critic. The inner critic isn't always accurate in its assertions (which helps put the critic in its place), and the thoughts that arise in the mind are not always true. This brings us to another life-altering bit of knowledge:

Our brains are wired to notice evidence that supports our beliefs and ignore evidence that doesn't.

So if I have a belief that I'm not worthy, my brain vigilantly notes situations that support that, whether it's true or not. (In the case of worthiness, it will never be true because everything has inherent worth.) It will see only evidence filtered through a belief bias and ignore evidence that's contrary to the belief. This can be troubling for those of us who were taught to believe they weren't worthy or valuable.

We can begin to "rewire" this tendency through actively becoming conscious of our strengths and value. We can consciously replace beliefs, particularly the ones we recognize as not true.

This process of unpacking and questioning each statement and belief can be quite revealing in recognizing the inner critic for who or what it is and the power it holds over us. Engaging directly with the inner critic is a guaranteed game changer, which leads us to the next approach—tracking and challenging its authority.

Engaging directly with the inner critic is a guaranteed game changer.

Judgments from the inner critic are usually learned elsewhere. With a more meticulous inquiry I discovered the original voice, which afforded me an opportunity to challenge its authority in my life. Harsh criticisms from my father, managers, teachers, and others continue to echo in the halls of my mind.

As these original sources are revealed, a more genuine kind and nurturing voice may emerge. The growing gap between thought and action can help us choose that voice to be the one that has authority in our belief system. This is the part of us that has our best interests at heart, knows the values we aspire to, and is big enough to see the lies our inner critic perpetuates.

One of my favorite techniques of working with the inner critic, and the one that creates the most spaciousness for me, is to *personify* the inner critic—to turn it into a character or even a caricature.

One of my coaching clients named her inner critic Dick Tate (dictate) when she recognized how much its demanding harshness ran her life. Another client named his Sir Awful A Lot, referring to his perspective on all situations. "Isn't this just awful!" This playful approach can be even more powerful by making an actual physical representation of the inner critic in whatever medium feels fitting.

Moving the inner critic outside the confines of our mind and purposefully engaging with it as an external object really helps grow the spaciousness between its assertions and our deeper knowing. This next exercise will help you flush out its claims more fully.

Exercise: Just Who Is My Inner Critic?

Begin an inquiry in your journal on each of the statements you discern from your inner critic. (Remember, the inner critic's voice is usually one of shame, blame, and extremes.) Then ask the following:

- What is the belief?
- Whom did I first hear this from? When was it? What was their statement? What were the circumstances?
- Is it true?
- If it's not true, what is a more accurate statement or belief?
- Create an affirmative statement from this greater truth and repeat it often.

As a final approach, we can choose to learn to have compassion for our inner critic. Critical attitudes and judgments usually come from hidden pain and fear. Wherever these beliefs originated, we can pretty much guarantee it was coming from fear or pain of some sort. Understanding this can evoke compassion and empathy, which again changes our relationship to the inner critic and how we receive their judgments. Rather than taking the statements seriously about ourselves, we can begin to see the suffering that must have been present when the originator of these statements began hurling these judgments towards us.

For me, one persistent critical thought is that I'm not worthy—that really, there is no room for me on the planet. I am the youngest of six kids. I was born prematurely to a smoking and drinking mother who was married to an abusive, alcoholic man—my father. The consistent beating down of my inherent goodness took its toll over the years, and to this day, that belief still haunts me, and usually at the most critical times.

Patiently over the years—and lovingly when I can remember—working with mindfulness, forgiveness, recovery principles and the inner-critic work discussed here, I have found a way to recognize just how much pain and fear my father experienced. Without making excuses for his and my mother's actions, I can genuinely hold them both in compassionate understanding. (It is also true this critical way of parenting was not the complete story, but this is what the mind holds onto most. I have to actively work to recollect the good times.)

With this compassionate attitude, I can more easily diffuse the pain that arises from hearing these inner thoughts, though sometimes I still get stung by them. I've accepted the fact that I will most likely have these thoughts continue to arise in my mind for the rest of my days, but mindfulness and compassion have provided the freedom to work with them differently than just allowing them to hammer me into painful acceptance of their assertions.

I've also learned from engaging directly with thoughts that painful energy arises, is maintained, and gets even stronger when I resist or oppose them. So my practice has become to fully accept and then really question thoughts that arise in awareness.

Treat thoughts as mere hypotheses—things to be explored, tested and acted upon only when validated as true.

It is difficult to extract thoughts from the emotions they stir, which speaks to the intricate richness of our inner life. A growing capacity to be with this rich complexity is one of the more beautifully faceted jewels we receive from our mindfulness practice. Discovering the relationship of thoughts and emotions is a subtle and pleasurable adventure and the next natural step in our exploration of mindfulness and inquiry.

Chapter 14

Befriending Emotions

Make a commitment to honor and respect your body by being willing to learn from the emotions that affect it, even if that simply means bringing your loving awareness to it . . . The essence of being a good listener—to yourself or to a dear friend—is simply allowing emotion to be expressed freely and honestly. Over time, your caring focus can change pain to compassion.

— Christiane Northrup, MD

Much like working with thoughts, bringing mindfulness to our emotional experience can lead to sincere, genuine healing, and freedom. Not in any way trying to change our emotions but learning how to be intimately present with them as they form and dissipate helps our mindfulness practice broaden and deepen. It also gives us another meaningful gift—learning *from* them.

To me, emotions are indicators of so many things: *anger* can help me know when my boundaries are being infringed upon; *laughter* points to what brings me joy; sorrowful tears of *mourning* reveals how deeply I've loved; and *fear* shows me what I value, what's truly important to me.

Just as we've experienced how breath, thoughts, and sensations in the body arise, take form, and pass away, our emotions are similar when experienced with the same kind and open attention. Ever-changing, they rarely hang around for long, though some may return frequently. Emotions come in waves—sometimes strong and clear, other times subtle, nebulous, and still others, indescribably sublime.

Like a strong warrior, our tender care and kind attention can companion us through the most difficult and tumultuous emotions and yet, in the next moment, create space for the subtler and joyous states. Our loving mindfulness strengthens our ability to create a container for it all.

Exercise: Can Feelings Be Forced?

Set a timer for two minutes. Steady your attention on your anchor and see if you can "make" yourself feel the emotion of joy.

Does the very act of trying to make yourself feel a particular way help it come about or prevent it?

Next, try remembering the last time you felt joy. Fill in your mind's eye as fully as you can the details of the situation. Include time of day, place, smells, sounds, and sensations. What feelings arise in you now as you remember?

What was the difference in trying to make yourself feel a certain way and remembering a situation when you were joyful?

Anyone who has fallen out of love can understand the concept that we can't force emotions. *Emotions* are temporary states of being that arise as a result of certain conditions, and while we can cultivate those conditions, we can't create the emotions themselves.

Sometimes something as simple as lifting the corners of our mouth upward can turn into the beginnings of an inner smile that can spread throughout our being.

> *We can foster, we can support, we can cultivate conditions, and then we let go. We can't force emotions into being.*

You may have experienced this truth when angry or hurt but forcefully, through clinched teeth, replied, "I'm fine!" when someone asked how you were. You may have forced an untrue answer, but the emotion was still seething under the surface.

There's a real blessing here. Richness and meaning come from experiencing things that arise naturally rather than contrived. Even so, cultivating conditions or creating the circumstances where things can arise for positive emotional states is a very real proposition.

Nurturing a container of acceptance, allowance, awareness, and compassion sets the stage for emotions, simple or complex, to arise and be fully felt and subsequently pass away. As we purposefully commit to lovingly accept our emotions, we set the stage for our emotional self to feel safe enough to arise unhindered without judgment.

In doing so, we prevent what is known as the *second arrow of suffering* from arising. The first arrow is the painful impact of an event itself—maybe it's illness, loss of a loved one, pain, or frustration from aging. The second arrow is the additional pain that is caused by pushing away, denying, or judging the situation. In other words, how we see and respond to the experience itself can create additional suffering. It's the second arrow—our response—that is in our hands.

As we ground our awareness in the present moment, opening to be with whatever is arising, we become less susceptible to additional suffering, fears, and hopelessness. If we feed catastrophic potentials, an anxious and nervous state will follow. If we come from a place of open acceptance, we experience a deeper intimacy with ourselves and our lives, fostering heartfelt connection and luxurious aliveness, regardless of whether the experience is positive, negative, or neutral.

We may have learned at an early age that painful emotions were to be avoided at all costs. We may spend much time and energy trying to block, avoid, or escape these difficult emotions. None of these approaches leads to less suffering in the long run. Quite the contrary, we'll actually be robbed of the opportunity to experience the depths of joy and love available in our lives as a result of this forceful approach.

We lose our potential to experience positive emotions when we try to force or repress any emotion.

This is because we are actively trying to control our situation rather than receiving and allowing it, and as you noticed earlier, we can't make an emotion happen.

Through kindhearted practice, fully meeting and allowing our emotions as they arise leads to less discomfort and more pleasantness. As researcher and author Brené Brown points out, "What we know now is that when we deny our emotion, it owns us." Accepting and allowing our emotions frees us from the pain and difficulty that arises from resistance. It expands our freedom and spaciousness in a way that is only available when we open to our full experience in an intentional, mindful, and loving way.

Some of my most difficult emotional experiences have actually become some of my most cherished. I've learned to savor them as once in a lifetime experiences—such as the pain I've felt from losing a loved one that reflects having loved so deeply; the anger from injustice that catapults me into action; or the realization that my physical and mental faculties are beginning to decline, leading to a reflection of the full and rich life I've lived. These are riches to cherish, not push away.

My family system helped me learn how to reach out to drugs and alcohol to numb my emotional pain and confusion. It was a very long, nasty, painful lesson. These "tools" I became so skilled in at a young age are not only ineffective and unnecessary; they were harmful to my body and robbed me of so many pleasant emotional experiences. I also lost the possibility of living to my full potential.

My psychological reactions to the dysfunction in my family were just telling the truth about the situation—it was painful, scary, and harmful. My emotions were literally a cry for help and an insistence for honesty about abuses to my heart, mind, and body. But learning how to stifle and stuff them turned out to be even more harmful and painful as years of emotional and physical self-abuse continued into my late thirties.

Early in recovery from codependency, after alcohol and other drugs faded from my repertoire of numbing tools, I committed to give up tobacco. It was the only substance I continued to use to numb my feelings.

Having quit smoking hundreds of times (and intending to do so and failing thousands more), my intimate partner at the time set a boundary around it, and I was ready. I had already tapered down to a few hand-rolled natural cigarettes a day. Being pushed over the edge by the threat of ending this budding relationship, I took the leap once again. I gave myself four uninterrupted days at the cabin to do anything I wanted and needed, *except* smoke tobacco.

The energy rushes during the first few days were extraordinary. I spent most of my time working on the wood pile—chainsawing, splitting, and hauling wood up the steep incline to the cabin. There were intense emotional rushes and astounding sexual arousal. I turned to eating chocolate (think of feel good endorphins and serotonin) and self-pleasuring, and since I couldn't reach out for my last crutch, tobacco, I was faced with using my mindfulness practice and recovery tools to help me through.

It was in that brief period that I sat down on the hillside time and time again to allow the flood of emotions and tears to undulate through my body. Surging waves of laughter, screaming, anger, fear, and the fierce withdrawal symptoms from twenty-five years of smoking were met straight on. I was committed.

By day five, the wild surging of withdrawal symptoms ceased. It's been over sixteen years now, and it's hardly possible for me to believe that I ever smoked. Just the thought of cigarette smoke causes my lungs to close down in defense.

In hindsight, interestingly enough, when I smoked, it offered me an opportunity to remove myself from a crowd or stop whatever activity I was engaged in and take a few deep breaths. I can only imagine the mixed messages my body received over the years from taking a break, relaxing, and breathing deeply while simultaneously polluting my lungs.

As the stormy waves subsided, subtle exhaustion, gentle energies and more tender emotions surfaced. My curiosity rose yet again: What was all the fuss about? Why was I stifling my most basic and natural reactions to life? How could they be bad or wrong?

Well, they weren't. There is nothing wrong with emotions—mine or others. They weren't "wrong." Stifling my emotions was how I survived a harmful, pain-filled dysfunctional family system and how I continued by reaching out for one dysfunctional relationship after another in my adult life.

Emotions reveal our values and boundaries.

Emotions are indicators when something is amiss, when something is sublimely right, and everything in between. Stifle one and you end up stifling them all. They are one of the most valuable tools we humans have to help us navigate through life and live by our precious principles. They are indispensable in our efforts to authentically befriend ourselves and anyone else.

Smothering emotions is like taking out the rudder
of life.

I committed right there and then to never consciously suppress my emotions again. Since childhood I was directed to believe most of my emotions were wrong. And they weren't. Time and again, they were telling me when something was terribly, terribly wrong.

Putting more credence and value on opinions from my family, my loved ones, and the community at large, I learned to become my own captor, carrying on the forceful shutting down of what makes me uniquely me, and the key to finding my own happiness.

Vulnerability is difficult without feeling safe.

Being on our own side helps shore up a sense of safety. Through creating a strong, compassionate container that includes receptivity and loving support, we are more likely able to open up to emotions in a deeply intimate way. It may be a long process to persuade them out of hiding, but with gentle, loving persistence and presence, this trail back to ourselves will lead to riches no ideal or imagined fantasy can touch.

Gently opening and staying present with our emotions is a practice. We must be careful that it doesn't become an exercise in stoicism or a lesson on accepting the unacceptable. We open to them and hear what we need to stay healthy, balanced, and thriving.

Just like with the breath, body sensations, or thoughts, practicing with our emotions isn't about controlling them, ignoring them, or invalidating them, basically disassociating from ourselves and our experience. It is about engaging in a more cherished and friendly way, patiently and lovingly as we would if a child we loved dearly were experiencing them.

When our practice includes the emotional body, our attention is aimed on staying present in the body as emotional energy expresses itself through waves of sensations—pulsing, tingling, pressure, constriction, movement, changing temperature—sometimes subtle, other times powerful, and still others overpowering.

As we become more aware of the intertwined dynamic relationship between thoughts, emotions, and sensations, we become more conscious of how they feed on one another and the potential for creating more pain—*the second arrow*. There are some techniques we can incorporate in our practice as supportive ways to help free us further.

Working with Difficult Emotions

> *Let everything happen to you. Beauty and*
> *terror. Just keep going. No feeling is final.*
>
> *— Rainer Maria Rilke*

There are times in virtually everyone's life when we feel engulfed and overwhelmed by emotions. If, like me, you are one who has spent many years suppressing feelings, shoring up your container to meet them with a little extra compassion and steadiness is helpful.

Another potent and loving tool is a process known by the acronym *RAIN*—recognize, allow, investigate, and natural or nurturing awareness. It is most challenging to reach for resources when are triggered or caught in a deep and difficult pattern. RAIN can help us bring a loving attention to these difficulties.

To practice with RAIN, try working with a situation that brings a slight annoyance, upset, anxiousness, or frustration just to get the feel for the process. When you are comfortable with the process, you can work with deeper frustrations and painful situations. Eventually, RAIN becomes an automatic go-to for dealing with difficulties.

Exercise: RAIN

Find a comfortable, alert posture and spend a few minutes settling with your core practice. Bring a situation that is troubling you into your awareness—maybe it's an annoyance with a behavior of yours, your partner, or a coworker. See yourself in the situation where you get stuck. Bring up the circumstances and details as best you can.

Let that moment when you are most caught come into view. See the specifics—maybe a verbal exchange or a behavioral act. Just see yourself in the situation. Allow yourself to respond to this situation as you would if it were happening. Maybe there's sadness or anger or fear. Just allow the details to fill in and respond as you would if it were actually happening. Then begin the practice of RAIN.

First, recognize. Notice that an emotional response has arisen; something is happening. Note the feeling tone of the emotion. Is it pleasant, unpleasant, neutral?

Next, allow. Pause and create a little spaciousness. Allow yourself to take the time and sit with the feeling, without needing to conceptually define it, change it, explain it, or justify it. Just let it unfold and be there as it is.

Then, begin an investigation of what is happening right now. Let go of the story and notice where in the body you feel it most. Go there with a kind interest and attention. What is the felt sense? See if you can name the sensations. Tightness, constriction, pain? Warm? Hot? Cold? Stabbing, gripping, throbbing? The investigation happens in the direct experience in the body and not the story.

Notice the natural awareness that arises from this shift of attention. What happens to the emotional state as you just let it be and turn to the investigation? Does it change? Does it lessen? Grow? Dissipate?

> Now bring a nurturing attention to the experience. What kindness can you bring to it? Maybe meet yourself and this difficulty by placing your hand to your heart and bringing some reassurance that you are here, mindful and caring. Maybe convey a tenderness and a kind attention—an intimate presence with what is—bringing to it a "yes" or "this too" and holding space for it within yourself and for yourself.

With RAIN, you are resting and holding yourself compassionately with your own kind attention, the larger spaciousness of your life, and the greater mystery of *all that is*.

RAIN can be a trusted friend on our journey through difficult emotional experiences, as can a few other tools. We can create a little room for our emotions through the use of *noting* as we learned with thoughts. A simple word softly in the background can help release the hold, as can breathing gently into the area of our body where the sensations are most uncomfortable or intense, as we learned with physical pain. Rather than running, condemning, or shutting down, these simple acts of kindness can create a gentle shift in our experience.

When difficult emotions are persistent we may want to explore what we can do to help solve the situation and take action. If there is nothing we can do to change things, as in the case of the death of a loved one, can we be present and open to the full experience in the compassionate field of our own heart? If not, can we enlist the assistance of a trusted friend who can hold a loving, nonjudgmental space with us as we allow ourselves to open fully to the pain? We may have to do this again and again as our mourning process unfolds, but through our considerate and steady attention, we have the power to companion ourselves through even the most difficult painful periods.

When Shyla died, I was curious what my emotional experience was going to be. Most of my meditation periods were spent just opening and holding space with my process. Sometimes it would be sharply painful, and other times sweet and tender.

*I had built a loving container to hold it all, and
I didn't want to miss a moment of it because I
was entering the next phase of one of the most
important relationships in my life.*

Being deeply touched by Shyla hasn't gone away because of her death. It's just changed, and my love for her is now expressed differently.

While we can do all we can to create this available container, there may be times when it's not appropriate to delve deeply into our emotions. Once during a resiliency training for an organization, some of the employees attending were less than hospitable to my presentation. The department was experiencing probably the most difficult time in its history because of a series of natural disasters and an extended period of staff transitions. At one of the early presentations, a few of the staff members with strong personalities were outright rude and contemptuous. I was wholly unprepared for the hostility toward the information I was sharing, and I was taken aback. It felt like *I* was being attacked.

Because of my history, I could instantly feel I was triggered and the fight, flight, or freeze zone of my brain was stepping in to take over. I was familiar enough with these sensations from the chemical reactions in my body to know what was happening and was able to get through the session. It was the last presentation of the day but knew I had to set aside time to really work through what had happened.

It wasn't until days later while sifting through the feedback surveys that it could sink in that this was really about two people and their own troubling situation and not about me or the material being presented.

Even though my presentation wasn't as optimum as I would like because of the triggering, mindfulness helped me stay present enough to finish it in a way that brought benefit to the attendees. (My inner critic was pretty strong in response, but my commitment and practice of compassionate self-care created the situation where I could do some deeper inquiry and healing at a more opportune time than during a client presentation.)

When it isn't appropriate, I vow to meet these emotions at another time and am sure to keep that commitment with myself, or it just becomes an exercise in invalidation.

As revealed earlier, research supports mindfulness as helpful for working with depression and anxiety. Since both of these conditions arise from the thinking mind, trying to think our way out of them may actually increase the grip they have on us.

Depression is usually accompanied by thoughts of the past, whereas anxiety can be triggered by fears of the future. The cycle can become quite debilitating, and the physiological reactions disconcerting. Mindfulness is now used as an antidote for these conditions, giving relief in the moment of a troubling episode and reducing the likelihood of future ones.

Instantly, when we bring attention to our present moment experience, an interruption to the flow of thoughts occurs. As we focus on the direct experience in the moment, the thinking mind is redirected from its course and can send important messages to the brain that we are okay. Over time, thanks to our practice, we can more easily disengage from the ruminating and catastrophizing mind—whether focused on the past or future—helping dissipate the painful line of thinking and reasoning.

Resourcing

The practice of allowing thoughts to arise while feeling the co-occurring sensations creates pause enough for us to discern our best course of action. We end up with access to a deeper place of wisdom than our survival brain.

I liken mindfulness to using a clutch in a car. When a clutch is out, the car is moving forward in whatever gear is engaged. When the clutch is pushed in, the gears still spin, but they're not engaged with the drive shaft, so the car doesn't move.

I see thoughts as the spinning gears; when the clutch is pushed in (when mindfulness is being used), the gears still spin (thoughts still happen), but the vehicle isn't moving (I'm not acting on the thoughts). With mindfulness, we make our decisions from a calm and centered driver's seat and choose when to release the clutch (take action).

During very challenging emotional or thinking states, when we can't even remember there is a clutch or when attention to physical sensations actually creates a rise in anxiety, another tool called *resourcing* can help.

When I was finishing my bachelor's degree at Sonoma State University, we had a very difficult semester that focused solely on the state of the environment. This was in 2006 when the evidence of climate change was irrefutable. Scenario after scenario of damage to our planet was presented each week in our readings. We learned how every natural living system on the planet was threatened and some on the verge of collapse. About two-thirds into the semester, most of us were depressed and struggling with these facts. Some of us reached out for counseling.

I attended my annual weeklong silent meditation retreat during Thanksgiving break. While we are instructed to not read during retreat, I had deadlines immediately following that included reading more material on the environment.

I usually sleep a lot during the first few days of retreat, my exhausted mind and body taking time to catch up. But when I read in the evenings, I noticed heart palpitations rise. These had been creeping up throughout the semester. This was anxiety from knowing the dire present condition of our planet and where we inevitably were heading if our behaviors didn't change.

In this case, bringing mindfulness to the sensations seemed to increase the heart palpitations. Paying such close attention set off my catastrophizing mind; I began thinking I maybe had a heart condition and needed medical attention. Or was I having an anxiety attack? Each inquiry caused my heart to race even more. Quite concerned, I met with my teacher who suggested the resource exercise. She was also quite adamant that I put down all reading during the retreat.

Practice: Resourcing

Resourcing involves bringing attention in and out of the area of intense discomfort a little bit at a time as a way to lessen an otherwise overwhelming experience. To do so, notice where in the body you're experiencing the difficulty, and rest your attention on the area for a brief period—maybe a breath or two. Then find another part of your body where the sensations are either neutral or pleasant and shift your attention there for a period. Then move your attention slowly toward the difficult sensations pausing at the very edge of it. Explore where the intensity begins and where it lessens. Notice what happens as you do. Keep exploring, and if it gets too intense, take another rest in a neutral or pleasant area.

Like with the body scan, practice moving your attention toward and away from the sensations, pausing briefly in each area of pleasant, neutral, and unpleasant. Then, explore bringing a loving and caring breath or two to the difficult areas and see what you notice.

This is a practice that may take time to even remember as a tool if you find yourself in a difficult emotional state. Overiding the amygdala in action is very difficult. Over time, though, this practice can serve you through challenging situations.

As I put down the reading at the retreat and focused on this practice, as well as continuing to catch up on rest, the heart palpitations subsided and I left the retreat relaxed, refreshed, and ready for the remaining weeks of the semester.

Fortunately, the final third of the course was focused on large and small scale actions underway to help turn things around. Outstanding innovative ideas and grassroots efforts were emerging to help transcend us out of our destructive habits.

As difficult as that semester was, it planted the seeds to launch a local food co-op in my hometown in hopes of shifting our local food system to a more sustainable one.

Another thing that acknowledges my reaction to a situation while lessening its intensity and my identification with it is remembering that difficult emotional states are not unique to me.

We all at one time or another experience the gamut of emotions.

This assurance helps create a compassionate spaciousness where I can practice replacing "I am afraid of" with "I am experiencing fearful thoughts about this" or "Here is fear, and this is how it is."

Keeping a tender attitude as we dive into our emotional body with these practices increases our potential for freedom. Committing to meeting ourselves with as much love, compassion, and understanding will surely open our hearts to creating a compassionate state to meet ourselves more fully.

Including Compassion
and Kindness

Chapter 15

Generating Forgiveness

Generally speaking, in the Buddhist tradition, compassion and loving kindness are seen as two sides of same thing. Compassion is said to be the empathetic wish that aspires to see the object of compassion, the sentient being, free from suffering. Loving kindness is the aspiration that wishes happiness upon others.

— His Holiness, the Fourteenth Dalai Lama of Tibet

Along with setting intentions and direction for our lives, we can add a few other simple, warmhearted exercises to our tool kit, namely, compassion and loving-kindness practices. Incorporating compassion and loving-kindness practices further serve to reconnect our hearts, bodies, and minds. Really, though, the practices cannot be separated because as we peel down to our essential nature, our natural tendencies toward kindness, compassion, and forgiveness are uncovered. Just like our breathing and our thinking, they happen naturally, *and* we can cultivate them for greater ease, comfort, health, and well-being.

Compassion and loving-kindness practices contribute to generating the happiness and joy we all seek to experience in life. First, we work to reveal and heal any lingering suffering through compassionate practices, such as *forgiveness*. Then we turn to loving-kindness practices, which give rise to happiness.

When we begin our mindfulness practices, areas of hurt or pain from situations and people in the past may surface. Taking time to see them with a compassionate heart lends itself to significant healing for ourselves and our relationships. The following practice can serve us in many ways to heal the past and support us forward.

Practice: Forgiveness

Give yourself a considerable amount of uninterrupted time for this practice to let the genuine images and feelings surface at their own pace.

Rest in kind awareness for a few minutes, allowing your thoughts to settle. Tenderly connecting with your heart, begin this practice with any harms or hurts you may have caused others. Since we all make mistakes and we all cause harm to others, from a place of kind acceptance, repeat to yourself:

"In these ways that I have caused harm to others, either knowingly or unknowingly, whether out of my own pain, fear, anger or confusion, I ask for forgiveness."

Allow the mental images of beings and situations to surface naturally as you recite this. With an open heart, ask each one for forgiveness.

"Please forgive me."

Next, extend this forgiveness to yourself for any self-created harm.

"In these ways I have caused harm to myself through abandonment, neglect, or harshness, whether in word, thought, or act, either knowingly or unknowingly, I forgive myself. Whether out of fear, pain, anger, or confusion, I forgive myself. I forgive myself."

Allow memories of self-hurt to surface, receiving them in a space of loving acceptance and cradling sympathy. We all do our best at any given moment. Take your time and meet them kindheartedly.

Lastly, you can extend forgiveness to others that may have hurt or harmed you.

"Remembering the many ways others have hurt or harmed me, whether out of fear, pain, confusion, or anger, I have carried this pain in my heart far too long. To the extent that I am able at this time, I offer you forgiveness. I extend to you forgiveness. I forgive you."

Give yourself plenty of time to meet the hurts with a gentle willingness to heal, holding a kind space with the heart as it finds its way to an opening.

For some, this practice may bring into awareness the deep hurts, anger, and pain that have long been buried. Touch this too, gently and without judgment. Forgiveness cannot be forced. Continue the practice, and over time, the words and images will gradually do their work.

Chapter 16

Cultivating Kindness and Well-being

As we learned earlier, loving-kindness exercises provide immediate relief from pain and emotional tension as well as increase our happiness set point. This powerful exercise is one of the easiest ways we can cultivate happier states of being in ourselves. It also has a mysterious impact on others whom we think about during our practice.

Practice: Loving-kindness

This practice can be added for the last five or so minutes of your regular mindfulness practice or practiced on its own. The more regular you are, the greater the benefits.

Consciously tune into the understanding that everyone wants happiness as you drop your attention to your heart area. While holding an intention of well wishing, much like you would when you extend birthday greetings to someone you really love, silently repeat over and over to yourself a few of these or other phrases that really resonate with your heart:

- May I be well.
- May I be peaceful and at ease in my mind.
- May I be vibrant and healthy in my body.
- May the conditions for joy and happiness in my life increase.
- May I experience meaningful and loving relationships.
- May I love well and may I be loved.
- May my sorrows and sufferings be lessened.
- May I be free from inner and outer harm. May I be safe.
- May I experience prosperity in health, wealth, and relations.
- May I be happy. May I be deeply, deeply happy.

The ideal is to practice this for thirty days holding only yourself in the cradle of love and well wishing. But if you notice a resistance or difficulty with wishing yourself well (maybe feelings of unworthiness, uncomfortableness, or selfishness arise as you do), gently remind yourself that everyone wants and deserves happiness, including you.

If you still find it too difficult, begin the practice by first thinking of a person or being with whom it is very easy for you to want good things for—maybe a child, loved one, or pet. Hold them in your heart-mind's eye while you repeat the phrases, extending kindness and well wishing to them. At the end, visualize them turning to you with heartfelt sincerity, offering, "May you, too, experience these things. May you, too, be happy." Cultivate receptivity to this kind outpouring, really letting it seep in.

After the first thirty days, you can include others in your circle of love—those whom it's easy for you to want good things for, those whom you may know only casually, those you have difficulties with, and, finally, all beings, known and unknown.

Forgiveness and loving-kindness practices begin a journey of healing the pains of our past, give us a new way to see ourselves and others, and set the course for a brighter tomorrow through training our brain toward happiness. As with all the mindfulness and supportive practices, they are simple but not always easy. Give yourself time and space to allow these gentle practices to sink into your being. This path is a lifelong one, and you are continually invited to meet yourself with an open and tender heart.

Clarifying Our Path
to Happiness

As the healing practices give way to more inner peace and emotional freedom, we turn our attention to personal clarity for growing our happiness and joy. The next few chapters help us dive deep, get clear and commit to our intentions.

Chapter 17

What are Our Deepest Intentions?

My happiness grows in direct proportion
to my acceptance and in inverse proportion to my
expectations.

— Michael J. Fox

Living with conscious intention is one of the most powerful and transformational things we can do to create a life we love. The process begins with an exploration of what we think we want—what will give us happiness and meaning—and finishes with clarification and commitment

It may seem obvious, but as we continue to work with mindfulness, a simple inquiry into what would make us happy tends to reveal some surprises, because we are peeling off conditioning and discovering more of our authentic nature.

Exercise: What Makes Me Happy?

Use your journal to brainstorm on the following questions. Don't hold back on this one, and don't edit anything out. With brainstorming, there are no wrong answers, and nothing is too big or small to include:

- What would make me happy? Loving relationships? Enough money? Travel? Fame? Education? Helping others? Excelling in my career?
- What brings me pleasure? Racing cars? Watching children play? Eating a tasty and sumptuous meal?
- What brings me joy?
- What gives me meaning? Challenge? Helping others? Cooking?
- What are my most favorite things to do? See? Enjoy? Eat?

Next, we'll take what we've learned from this exercise and distill it down to the very essence of what we think we're looking for.

Exercise: Distilling It to the Essence

Use your answers from above and brainstorm around these questions:

- What would I have if I had or did these things? Fun? A new car? A nice home? No pain in the body?
- What would this give me? What are the feelings I will experience as a result? Peace? Joy?

Contentment? Excitement? Fulfillment? No fear?
Rest?
- Why are these important to me?

As an example, here's the work I did in just one area of my life—a new home:

- What will I receive if I attain this goal/vision?
  - Peace of mind knowing that Shyla will be in comfort
  - More time to pursue other things than the basic necessities of living
  - More ease in my daily routine

- What are the *feelings* I will experience as a result?
  - Calm
  - Comfort
  - Ease
  - Assuredness
  - Joy
  - Safety
  - Trust

- Why are these important to me?
  - I love Shyla and want her to be comfortable in her final years.
  - My body is getting tired of the continual strenuous work it takes to live on a daily basis.
  - There is something bigger calling me at this time.

Getting clear on *what* we want and *why* we want it prepares us to be clearer of our intentions and more strategic with our actions. What we learn through the distilling exercise helps us break free from the *expectation trap*. Plus, it opens us to greater possibilities for receiving what we are really wanting from reaching our vision—the experience and feelings.

There are many ways I can feel calm, safe, and at ease, and that's what I was really looking for in my move to a new home. I actually had opportunities to experience these feelings along the way to securing my home. If I hadn't done this exercise first, I would have been stuck thinking I would never feel peace, ease, and comfort *until* I moved into the perfect home. I would have focused on having the specific details of the home rather than being open to receiving comfort, peace, and ease now.

It took us a year and a half to move into our new house. Many possibilities came together and fell apart, came together and fell apart, and came together and fell apart. If it wasn't the funding, the offers weren't accepted. Or I couldn't buy in a particular neighborhood because they didn't have municipal water. Or there was nothing available in my price range by the time I qualified for a loan. And on and on.

All the while, though, I could feel the energy moving us down the hill. Box after box seemed to magically get packed and toted down the hill where I stored it on a pallet under a tarp. As the nights turned colder and Shyla's energy slowed down, I was willing to settle for a less than optimum place and willing to rent, even though the market at the time made it more affordable to purchase. But I continued on in trust, focusing on staying present and open to receiving joy, calm, comfort, and assuredness as I went.

Chapter 18

Setting Our Compass

In order to carry a positive action, we must develop here a positive vision.

— *His Holiness, the Fourteenth Dalai Lama of Tibet*

Now that we've distilled our heart's deepest calling to the essence, it's time to pull all that together in a concise and powerful *vision statement*. A vision statement is an inspiring, positively oriented, clear picture of the future we want to create. It communicates goals and aspirations, and in doing so, it clarifies and sets our direction. It sets our compass.

Exercise: Drafting a Vision Statement

Look back over the previous exercises and see if you can pull out the most important parts of what you're wanting. Compile them into a few meaningful sentences.

Here is a first draft vision statement for my new home:

Shyla and I live comfortably and peacefully in an easily accessible, affordable, and nurturing home. We rest in safety, trust, and joy with plenty of time to do things we love. We live in effortless vibrancy.

Notice the adjectives came from the feelings I explored in the distilling exercise. Also, when I expressed something in the negative during brainstorming, such as my body getting tired, I reoriented it toward the positive—we live in effortless vibrancy.

The vision statement is positive, present tense, and filled with what we'll receive when we reach it. Now it's your turn.

Focusing on the essence—what we'll experience and feel—makes it pretty clear there are lots of options to fulfill this vision, and yet it's really clear what we're wanting. Once we're clear on our direction, our vision, we're ready to step into commitment.

Chapter 19

Stepping into Commitment

Courage is the commitment to begin without any guarantee of success.

— JoHann Wolfgang von Goethelf

If you felt a little quiver in your stomach when you read it was time to commit, then you're not alone. Many of us get at least a little nervous when it comes to *commitment*. A commitment is really just devoting ourselves to a cause or an activity that has meaning for us. It's a natural next step and reflects a dedicated undertaking toward our deepest desires. Commitment is then reinforced with our actions.

Desire → Intention → Commitment → Action

When you create a vision that aligns with your heart, mind, and body, commitment is really just stepping into the real you—the best *you*. Commitment is a powerful choice to trust in yourself and your vision.

Even though your vision aligns with your deepest intention for yourself, you may get nervous because you may not know how to make it happen. That's okay! We're just committing to move forward in a particular direction—toward our heart's desire.

Remember the difference between intention and expectation? We're at the intention part. We're setting a compass direction and taking the first step, being as clear and present as possible. We don't know, ultimately, where it will take us, and we'll probably navigate through a few course corrections, but we're dedicated to the intention and are stepping into action through commitment.

> *You always have two choices: your commitment versus your fear.*
>
> *—Sammy Davis Jr.*

If your vision is highly attuned with your values and your heart's deeper calling, your commitment just about makes itself. *Of course* you're going to head in that direction. *Of course* you're going to take those next steps.

On the way, as obstacles and life circumstances create hurdles (and they most undoubtedly will) our commitment says, "I'm willing to take a look at anything that is getting in my way."

The commitment equates to becoming unstoppable, or as one client puts it, "I'm not going to stop trying."

> *Commitment is an act, not a word.*
>
> *—Jean-Paul Sartre*

Are you ready?

Exercise: Standing in Commitment

Look at your vision statement and consider what your level of commitment is. Now, scale it between 10% - 100%.

Create a line on the floor with a scarf or other object. On your side of the line is the land of whatever percent of commitment you know you're resting in. On the other side of the line is the land of 120% commitment. When you're ready, step from your level of commitment to the land of 120%.

How does it feel? Are you excited? At ease? What did you notice in your experience about making the commitment? Nervousness? Fear? Excitement? A big "Yes!"?

Now lift the scarf or object off the floor and allow the land of 120% commitment to fill the whole space. Imagine it expanding beyond all walls to fill all time and space so that anywhere you are, you are living in the land of 120% commitment.

Reflect in your journal about this experience.

Chapter 20

Support Along the Way

*Belief consists in accepting the affirmations
of the soul; unbelief, in denying them.*

— Ralph Waldo Emerson

With your vision in place and your commitment undertaken, the next step for living the life you intend is to support your efforts on a regular basis. Reading and speaking your vision statement often (and refining it as you grow and gain new insights) will affirm your intention. Creating other supportive statements that affirmatively assert your intention can help even more.

Statements of affirmation are written and spoken in the present tense from a place of gratitude. This is because we have already clarified, set, and committed to our intention and vision and we're just on our way there. Once we've done this, it's just a matter of the path unfolding, *even if we can't see the path all the time and we haven't seen the path all the way to the vision.* We have, though, taken the first step on the path. We are on our way to this destination of meaning and fulfillment, and for that, we can be grateful.

Here are some good phrases you can use to help you craft statements of affirmation:

- Thank you that . . .
- Perfect-for-me
- This or something even better
- I am extremely happy with the outcome
- For the highest good and truth of all concerned

Here are few examples I used for finding our new home:

- Thank you that I am living in the perfect-for-me home that meets all of my and Shyla's needs.
- Thank you for the comfort, beauty, peace, and joy Shyla and I enjoy together in our easily affordable and accessible beautiful and nurturing home.
- I am extremely happy with our new home.

That last statement was given to me by a friend who offered us supportive thoughts. When I shared what I was looking for, he said, "Rather than remember all the particulars, how about if I just see you extremely happy with the outcome and we'll let the universe attend to the details?" How perfect! It ideally situates us in the intention space. There are many homes that could meet our needs and make us happy. And frankly, there's far more intelligence in the universe about what would make me happy than I can hold in my limited mind. I can't see what's up around the corner on the path to my vision, but I'm sure clear when I reach it—because I'll experience great feelings of "Yes!" I'll know it deep in my soul.

The most powerful affirmation doesn't come from the conscious mind but from your Soul, an affirmation in which you are not trying to convince yourself of something you don't believe, but rather you are becoming aware of the truth and the reality of what you truly are.

— Dragos Bratasanu

Exercise: Statements of Affirmation

Pulling from the phrases and examples above, take your vision statement and write a few affirmative statements that will support your intention and direction. Keep it positive, thankful, and in the present tense.

Commit to reading the affirmative statements at least once a day for the next thirty days.

Reflect in your journal about this experience and what you notice along the way. What was the outcome at the end of the thirty days?

As we continue our mindfulness practices and the path toward our emerging vision, it is likely we will experience shifting and changing desires and ideas. Feel free to refresh and rewrite your vision and affirmative statements to best reflect this new understanding. The process is flexible and meant to be supportive of your growing awareness, emerging authenticity, and deeper connection with your heart's calling.

As we stay grounded in loving awareness, we may be pleasantly surprised to discover when we're actually living parts of our vision. This is a good time to become even more embodied, so we can experience the delicious fruits of our path.

Mindfulness brings a more tangible richness and aliveness to all we experience, so it's also important that we celebrate anything that shows our progress. Celebrating is a way of consciously acknowledging our advancement. It gives us continued hope, strength, and courage. It also helps rewire the negativity bias as we bring our focus to the more positive and pleasant experiences.

There is no celebration too small.

Our celebrations don't need to be show-stopping or all-out razzle-dazzle explosive ones. The point is to become conscious of our accomplishments and to drink that experience—the acknowledgement—into our being and awareness.

Actively cocreating deep meaning and joy for ourselves will not only make us more happy, but it will also contribute to the larger field of conditions and circumstances that others experience and feel because *moods are contagious*—positive ones even more so.

Our growing joy and happiness will affect those in our sphere. And those people will then affect those in their sphere. In this way, ripples of contentment and joy and fulfillment will gently move outward from our willingness to risk and step into a life of deep fulfillment. And it all begins inward. As we experience more of these positive things in our lives, that ripple effect will will bring more positivity to the world.

When there is inner peace, there's a chance for outer peace.

Deepening Compassion and Kindness

Chapter 21

Additional Compassion Practices

If you want others to be happy, practice compassion. If you want to be happy, practice compassion.

— His Holiness, the Fourteenth Dalai Lama of Tibet

Compassion is at the core of our mindfulness practice not only because of its impact on our wellness, health, and happiness but also because it impacts all we do and all we touch. At a time when hatred and grievances are being actively cultivated in the larger world as a means to an end, practicing compassion becomes all the more important.

In particular, compassion gives us solace in difficult times, helps heal wounds, and strengthens our capacity to respond to life's challenges from our heartfelt and intended values.

Compassion offers us a way out of the painful spiral of divisive discourse.

Knowing that we all are subject to the countless challenges life offers, we can learn to build a sense of camaraderie with others with the assistance of a few practices.

Practice: Just Like Me

Recognizing how we are more alike than different fosters a sense of compassion and caring for others. The practice is similar to loving-kindness where we inwardly recite simple phrases with another in mind.

Either when meeting someone for the first time, when connecting with someone you know, or when you find yourself having difficulties or differences with someone you love and care about, you can use these phrases as you hold them in your heart-mind's eye:

- Just like me, this person is seeking happiness in their life.
- Just like me, this person is trying to avoid suffering in their life.
- Just like me, this person has known sadness, loneliness, and despair.
- Just like me, this person is seeking to fill their needs.
- Just like me, this person is wanting to feel loved and accepted.
- Just like me, this person is learning about life.

Modify the phrases as they work best for you and the situation and repeat as often as you'd like.

Have you ever had the experience where a complete stranger acts out in anger toward you? Or a coworker all of a sudden verbally attacks you? You may take it personally and respond back with anger, or you may walk away stunned and confused about what you did to cause this. When we are met with anger and unkindness, it is easy to respond in kind. Our fight, flight, or freeze system may be evoked, and without thinking, we may lash out in retaliatory anger or walk away grumbling.

Just taking a moment to consciously remember how we ourselves automatically react to situations such as these can help us better understand and have compassion for what could be behind the anger of others we meet. We can take this even further through a thoughtful inquiry exercise.

Practice: What's Beneath This Anger?

The next time someone meets you with anger or other unpleasant attitude, first, invite in a mindful pause by taking a deep breath. Then look to discover what's beneath it. With a stranger passing or driving by, you may have to use your imagination of what could be happening in their life at that moment. Maybe someone they love is ill or hurt, maybe they just lost their job, maybe they ended a relationship, or maybe their children are having difficulties. Maybe they had a difficult childhood full of pain and suffering.

It is like the story of the young woman walking in a forest when a fierce wolf leaps out to attack. Frightened, she leaps back. But as she looks closer, she notices that the wolf's back paw is caught in a trap. When we see anger in others, they may be caught and trapped in a painful situation.

If it's someone you know, you may want to take the time to ask. Sometimes they may not be aware that they are responding with irritation and hostility. Digging beneath the anger can help reveal a deeper need or calling for help. Is there something you can do to help them or the situation? Sometimes just compassionately listening and validating someone's experience is enough to shift and help disperse a biting attitude.

If you aren't able to take a mindful pause during the situation, take time later when you are calm and more detached from the event to reflect. Using this exercise cannot only help us and the other understand differently, but bringing a loving awareness to the situation may also help prevent a cycle of ongoing anger and hurt with those we love and care for.

Practice: Self-Compassion Break

This practice is from self-compassion expert Dr. Kristin Neff and based on the three aspects of self-compassion. It can be used when you find yourself in a difficult situation or on its own by calling up a trying situation from the past.

First, when we recognize that we are suffering, we can silently repeat one of these phrases:

- This is a moment of suffering.
- This moment is really hard.
- This is a difficult struggle.

We then recognize that we are not exempt from struggle or suffering in this life. Everyone experiences it, even though it may come in different forms for each of us. We can remember this through repeating one of these phrases:

- Suffering is a part of life. No one is exempt.
- Struggles are a part of life. No one is exempt.
- Difficult moments are a part of life. No one is exempt.

Finally, we bring a tender compassionate response to our plight with repeating one of these phrases:

- May I be kind to myself in this moment.
- May I meet myself with compassionate care.
- May I love and accept myself in this moment.

Add a little more comfort and care to this practice by placing your hands on your heart or other part of your body, with a soothing intention. Take time to open up to the feelings in the body and receive this loving compassionate self-care.

Working with compassion and loving-kindness practices increases our happiness, connection, and love in our hearts. It soothes the mind and has positive reverberations in our body. These practices have the capacity to shift who we are in the world as well as everyone we touch. Compassion for self and others is a simple yet powerful way to affect change on the planet.

Companioning
Us Onward

Chapter 22

Supportive Mind, Supportive Action

The Veil

There are moments when the veil seems almost to lift, and we understand what the earth is meant to mean to us—the trees in their docility, the hills in their patience, the flowers and the vines in their wild, sweet vitality. Then the Word is within us, and the Book is put away.

—Mary Oliver

There is a blissful dynamic experience and sublime knowledge available to us when we take on mindfulness and compassion practices. Listen carefully and take action on what you hear. Through the teachings and exercises in this book, you've taken the seat for yourself and experienced directly how these practices can transform your life.

Maybe your practice revealed some unfinished business of the past, and the journey now includes one of healing the heart. Maybe you've found a renewed sense of joy and purpose. Maybe a combination. In any case, you can choose to embark on a lifelong journey of new depths and dimensions to what it means to be human at this time.

As your practice continues, your ability to choose how to respond to life and its myriad situations from a more deeply aligned mind, body, and heart is strengthened. You've most likely experienced a growing reconnection of these vital parts of your being that were separated through conditioning and circumstance.

You hopefully have more access to your innate compassion for yourself and others, and you've learned how to get intentional to grow your joy and happiness. You've probably reconnected with and possibly redefined the values you use as guideposts for your life.

You've most likely discovered a deeper wisdom that is eager to guide you lovingly to greater inner peace, love, and joy.

Further, establishing a strong link with your emotional body bonds you to the complexity and richness of life's varied experiences, offering a more meaningful life.

These are no easy tasks, but the more you practice, the easier and more natural it all becomes. You are boldly forging a new trail in your biology, heart, and life. Each trek inward creates a clearer pathway. Each excursion helps you recognize the trail and signposts more easily until, over time, you can effortlessly glide into handling situations that used to concern and confuse you and experience more profound joys than you ever thought possible.

You've looked deeply inward to discover the passion within and garnered the courage to make strong commitments and take bold steps toward unleashing this evolving spiritedness. You may have discovered things you never knew about yourself or maybe just became more assured of what you know to be true about yourself.

You've undertaken a journey where there is no return. Your perceptions and experiences have shifted your way of thinking, and that shift will continue to grow. You've planted and cultivated seeds of an open heart and mind that are sprouting into precious and delicate shoots requiring regular tending, support, and care.

What is left? A continual connection with these practices will grow a kind and awakened heart. The more we cultivate these positive states of being, the more they rewire our brain, and the more they become our new habits. We are shifting our attention from the unconscious ruminating and catastrophizing mind to more conscious positive states of being situated in the present moment.

What the mind and heart frequently dwell upon becomes its inclination.

You've learned that you're not alone in suffering and that a lot of suffering comes from wanting things to be different. When we engage with things as they are, there is less pain and suffering and more helpful resources at hand. Wisdom, compassion, and insight become more readily available.

You've gained spaciousness and freedom from emotional suffering just from the simple act of bringing awareness to your situations. Knowing that your attitude and reactivity can color your experience, you now recognize that freedom and happiness are not conditioned by what is happening around you but rather how you relate to it.

By slowing down and seeing clearly, you've discovered how the cloudiness of a busy mind can settle, how natural compassion can arise, and how your connection to others can deepen. You've seen how taking small active steps can shift your experience.

And while habits endure, mindfulness is available in any moment.

You're learning that whatever is happening, you can trust in some deep way that mindfulness and kindness are here to help you. If you continue cultivating curiosity and kindness toward what you meet, and forgiveness to yourself when you act unmindfully, not only does your experience shift but your mindfulness becomes even more powerful.

From here, besides your resolve and commitment, some additional supports can help you maintain and expand your practice.

> *The most helpful thing you can do is to continue to see for yourself.*

No one else can give you the benefits of these practices. They must be gathered through your own effort.

Keeping a daily practice becomes as important as feeding ourselves. Most of us with a steady practice notice a marked difference when we miss it for even a few days. Building in brief mindfulness breaks into our day can help keep our intentions and connection to the practice fresh.

If you find yourself uncovering deep trauma along the way, the most kind and compassionate response would be to seek additional support and comfort through counseling or other trauma-release work, such as *emotional freedom technique* (EFT) or *trauma release exercises* (TRE). We each are worthy of the freedom healing brings.

My practice is most always more grounded and clear when I'm sitting with others. Finding companionship through mindfulness practice groups or support buddies is one of the more important ways we can buoy and bolster our practice. If you are interested in the Buddhist tradition, seek a local or online *sangha.*[47] Otherwise, there are growing opportunities through mindfulness groups and even guidelines for starting your own.[48]

These are just a few ideas to help shepherd your newfound practice. As a final support, you are invited to learn how to sit with the reliable majesty of an enormous mountain amid the ever-changing seasons of life. If you find resonance and connection with the mountain, use it in

---

[47] http://www.mindfulnessbell.org/directory/ or http://www.buddhistinsightnetwork.org/sanghas

[48] https://www.tarabrach.com/start-mindfulness-meditation-group/

your practice as it serves you. Learn to sit with its resolve, allowing a deep settling and stillness to seep in.

Practice: Mountain Meditation

Find yourself seated with dignity and grace, connecting to your core practice for a few minutes. Cultivate a comfortable but alert posture where you are stable, alert, and relaxed.

Beginning with your feet, bring your attention to the points of contact your body has with a surface. Sense how you are grounded and connected with the earth through this surface. Next, include your legs and hips, noticing how they, too, are connected to the earth. Allow your attention to slowly move up your body—hips to torso and upper body. Feel the connection and steadiness through your arms, shoulders, neck, and head.

Notice the stillness forming and take a moment to set an intention of dignity and resolve, like that of a stately and dignified mountain. Feel the connection that helps you know you are complete and whole in this moment.

Picture in your mind's eye a beautiful mountain—one you've seen in person or one you can imagine. Take a moment to gain a sense of this mountain. Maybe it has lofty peaks and a large base rooted in bedrock. Maybe it is steep or filled with gentle slopes. See its solid nature. Notice its massive, unmoving essence.

What other features do you see with this mountain? Snow? Trees? Granite? Streams? Waterfalls? Peaks and valleys? Allow your mind's eye to behold this noble, amazing form in all its splendor.

Next, visualize the mountain moving into your own body so you and the mountain are one. Share its statuesque stillness and solidity. See your head as its tallest peak, your shoulders and arms as its sides, your bottom and legs as its solid base rising from the depths of the center of the earth.

Notice, too, its aliveness as you experience each breath. Become the breathing mountain. Centered. Grounded. An unmoving presence yet a presence that supports life in its many forms—trees, birds, animals, lichen, and other plants. Vitally alive.

Watch as the sun travels across the sky from morning until night. Colors change. Aliveness can be seen all across the mountain as things come to life with the day. Night follows day, and things settle down. Day follows night, night follows day, and the mountain just sits, receiving it all, though things are constantly changing throughout. Now see through the seasons—summer brings deep greens; fall brings shifting colors; winter, snow, ice, and dormancy; and spring brings new life. With a mountain this size, any season can bring rain or fog. See it. Feel it. Watch the seasons come and go, again and again.

People come and visit the mountain and have their experience—awe, anger, fear, joy; the mountain remains the same, just being itself. Violent storms, snow, and rain come and go, and the mountain sits, receiving it all.

Year after year, spring comes and trees leaf out, flowers bloom, birds nest and sing, streams flow, and the mountain sits unmoved, remaining its essential self, even with the ebb and flow of movement on the surface.

Embodying the same central groundedness as the mountain, become constantly aware of the changing nature of your body and mind—periods of light and darkness, color and drabness, storms in your inner and outer world. We all endure periods of darkness and pain, joy, and uplift. Our appearance changes, too. By becoming the mountain, we can link up with its strength and stability and adopt its characteristics as our own, encountering each moment with mindfulness, equanimity, and clarity.

We can see our thoughts, feelings, and preoccupations; our crises; and the things that happen to us. We can see all these like the weather and seasons on the mountain.

We seem to take it personally, but its deeper characteristic is that it is impersonal. Our emotional encounters are not to be ignored or denied but to be encountered, honored, felt, and known for what they are. In this, we come to know a deeper silence, stillness, and wisdom. This is the wisdom we learn from magnificent and resplendent mountains. Enjoy this time sitting as the mountain.

Final Reflection

Drink your tea slowly and reverently . . .
As if it is the axis on which the earth revolves.
Slowly, evenly, without rushing toward the future.
Live the actual moment. Only this moment is life.

When you touch one thing with deep awareness, you touch everything. When you touch one moment with deep awareness, you touch all moments.

— Ven. Thich Nhat Hanh

To keep the miraculous mystery alive in your life, court the unique essence of your being that is emerging in every moment. There is only one you that can be experienced and expressed in life, and you only get this moment to meet that specialness that is distinctly yours. Giving up the opportunity to experience and express it can be seen as a tragedy in life. And in that vein, I offer you this reminder from Rumi.

I SWEAR MY DEAR SON
Jelaluddin Balkhi Rumi

I swear my dear son
no one in the entire world
is as precious as you are

look at that mirror
take a good look at yourself
who else is there above and beyond you

now give yourself a kiss
and with sweet whispers
fill your ears to the brim

watch for all that beauty
reflecting from you
and sing a love song to your existence

you can never overdo
praising your own soul
you can never over-pamper your heart

you are both
the father and the son
the sugar and the sugar cane

who else but you
please tell me who else
can ever take your place

now give yourself a smile
what is the worth of a diamond
if it doesn't shine

how can I ever put a price
on the diamond that you are
you are the entire treasure of the house

you and your shadow
are forever present in this world
you're that glorious bird of paradise

Acknowledgments
and Dedication

Acknowledgment of Teachers

So much of my work and practice comes from the many teachers and ancient wisdom texts I rely upon on a daily basis. Without them, I would surely lose my way. With them, I have learned to temper and occasionally laugh at my ego—or at least not let it run the show all the time.

I'm cultivating what I've come to know as *wholesome thinking*. Whether this is my true nature, revealing itself eventually through enough practice, I am not sure. But I know for sure whatever I cultivate becomes stronger in my being. I also know that by undertaking the additional practices (sometimes known as *precepts*) of nonharming, mindful speech, mindful action, mindful consumption, and mindful sexual conduct, I'm given a basic compass in life to help guide me away from preventable heartache and distress and toward more joy, love, and wisdom.

When I asked Ajahn Amaro, one of my favorite Buddhist teaching monks, whether we need to take these precepts since our true nature will be revealed through practice anyway, he assured me that we do.

Stopping destructive actions naturally gives rise to our true nature.

Until we do, our *karma* continues to slap us in the face with the repercussions of our harmful behaviors. I've since come to experience that they do go hand in hand. Practice *and* active nonharming give rise to our true nature.

> *First, we stop the pain. Then we grow the joy.*

And as my friend Nancy put it, "Not having received tools for loving, it can be awkward and take a lot of prethought at first. But after a while, it accesses my hidden automatic loving responses."

Consulting guides of wisdom on a regular basis helps me overcome my early conditioning and the ego's unceasing desires. Some of my favorites are the *Tao Te Ching* by Lao Tsu, translated by Gia-Fu Feng and Jane English; anything by Kahlil Gibran; the *I Ching* by Brian Browne Walker; and *The Couple's Tao Te Ching: Ancient Advice for Modern Lovers* by William Martin.

The latter helps keep my love in relationship with Jim fresh and in the moment. It also helps me let go of expectations and pictures of what I think intimate relationship and partnership *should* look like. Our relationship is another great and humbling teacher. Through Jim's continued willingness to bring his emotional availability to every situation—difficult or joyful—I continue to learn how to deepen love for myself and others. There are many simple gestures he extends that fill me with tender love. His gentle sense of humor also helps create spaciousness in times I'm stuck in past patterns.

Three overarching "teachers"—insight meditation (mindfulness), psychology, and recovery—have been the cornerstones of my life now for decades.

My heart was brought to this path firstly through a ten-day silent *Vipassana* meditation retreat in the early 1990s. It was a profound experience given that I wasn't able to sit for five seconds to that point. As I've mentioned before, because of my traumatic upbringing and addictions, a deeper psychological healing was needed either before or simultaneous to undertaking these practices. While I was completely blown apart with experiencing the contents of my mind and much revealed trauma, I came through it with a very clear understanding that I was capable of doing anything I put my mind to. Having great difficulty with anything other than immediate gratification, my capacity for self-discipline astounded me.

It took many years of painful attempts with the practice from those initial teachings before I fell to my bottom and landed in recovery—first for codependency, then my adult child issues, and finally for my own alcoholic/addict behaviors. The 12 Step recovery approach is another vitally important teacher, helping me learn how to live a healthier, spiritually oriented life.

My second exposure to insight meditation was at Spirit Rock Meditation Center with Jack Kornfield, a founding teacher and still my most favored. His works incorporate the badly needed psychological and compassion components that address the devastation I experienced in childhood. His teachings helped me quickly cut through the blocks I regularly bumped up against in my practice. In a matter of mere months, the convergence of his teachings and my recovery work helped catapult my practice to a more loving and kind one.

I'm am forever indebted to Jack Kornfield for introducing a way to live with heart, love, and self-compassion—particularly because I never thought myself worthy of these. Today, his ethics and style continue to guide me not only in my personal practices but also in my role as a teacher.

I regularly turn to other teachers—Tara Brach, Mark Coleman, Kevin Griffin, Teja Bell, and Anne Cushman—as their heart, humor, and ability to articulate the teachings inspire me.

I'm deeply indebted to His Holiness, the Dalai Lama, whom I've witnessed as the most solid embodiment of compassion, wisdom, and joy. I seek his perspective and guidance on a regular basis, particularly for political, national, or international events.

Thanks to the generosity of my partner, Jim Leonardis, and the freely offered teachings at Wat Pa Tam Wua in Thailand, I've been fortunate enough to take two brief retreats at the seat of my wisdom tradition, Theravada Thai Forest Insight Meditation, as well as to visit hundreds of *wats* (monasteries) throughout Thailand, Myanmar, and Cambodia.

There are two other teachers who stand out equally to those above for how they live and embody the teachings. First, Walter Robinson, whose property I shared for my ten-plus year adventure in voluntary simplicity. His every moment and movement was a striking awakening, and I forever cherish him.

Second, my canine companion, Shyla. Her dignity and poise as my protector in the wild and her gradual aging and death were the epitome of graceful, powerful living.

Finally, *Grace*—that ever-elegant mysterious and benevolent nature of the *All That Is,* revealing itself now and again with its startling and always humbling, sometimes last-minute rescues. I recently read how *mercy* is not getting what we truly deserve and *grace* is getting what we don't deserve. It is between these two I dance my life.

Dedication of Merit

It is common in the Buddhist tradition to dedicate any benefits accumulated from one's practice or life to all sentient beings—that they may be free from suffering. In the off chance that any drop of merit is gained from this book, from times of sitting in mindful awareness (as scattered and untrained this mind may be), and from my role as a teacher, may it be dedicated to all beings, particularly elephants, who suffer for the sake of human entertainment.

May all animals and humans be free from suffering—free for self-determination and authentic expression; free to be in natural beauty and splendor; free from oppression, harm, and exploitation. May they be cherished and held in high esteem.

Index

CPSIA information can be obtained
at www.ICGtesting.com
Printed in the USA
LVHW08*1955020818
585750LV00007B/67/P